A Fragile Enterprise

A Fragile Enterprise

Yesterday's Schools and Tomorrow's Students

Nancy Brigham

To Christine with affection + respect. Nancy

ROWMAN & LITTLEFIELD
Lanham • Boulder • New York • London

Published by Rowman & Littlefield
An imprint of The Rowman & Littlefield Publishing Group, Inc.
4501 Forbes Boulevard, Suite 200, Lanham, Maryland 20706
www.rowman.com

6 Tinworth Street, London SE11 5AL, United Kingdom

British Library Cataloguing in Publication Information Available

Library of Congress Cataloging-in-Publication Data
Names: Brigham, Nancy, 1934- author.
Title: A fragile enterprise : yesterday's schools and tomorrow's students / Nancy
Brigham.
Description: Lanham, Maryland : Rowman & Littlefield, 2019. | Includes bibliographical
references.
Identifiers: LCCN 2018046486 (print) | LCCN 2018060891 (ebook) | ISBN
9781475846034 (electronic) | ISBN 9781475846010 (cloth : alk. paper)
Subjects: LCSH: Educational equalization—United States. | Children with social
disabilities—Education—United States. | Public schools—United States.
Classification: LCC LC213.2 (ebook) | LCC LC213.2 .B744 2019 (print) | DDC
371.90973—dc23
LC record available at https://lccn.loc.gov/2018046486

Printed in the United States of America

For my children and grandchildren and
for all the other children whose lives
have touched and enriched mine.

Disclaimer

The chapters in this book report true events, gleaned from contemporaneous notes, unpublished reports, and from memory. In order to maintain anonymity, I have changed the names of individuals, schools, and school districts.

Contents

Preface

This book recounts my journey through a long career of evaluating public education in schools across the United States. Over thirty-five years, I have interviewed some five thousand teachers and observed instruction in hundreds of classrooms. I have assessed dozens of new programs to see if they improve education for poor and struggling students.

I have followed dozens of students through their school days and talked with their families about their hopes and dreams for their children. I have seen the system through the eyes of the powerless because, although parents and students are the customers of the education system, they have little or no voice in it.

I am the outsider who spends days or even weeks inside a school, sometimes exhilarated, sometimes discouraged, but never bored. The schools I visit are poor, the children I observe often have disabilities, and their families may not speak English very well.

Along the way, I have met principals who inspire their teachers and some who barricade themselves inside their offices, apparently hoping the school will run by itself. I have observed teachers who were so bad that I wanted to make a citizen's arrest and some so incredibly good that I actually broke out in goose bumps.

I have never met a student's family, no matter how poor, who did not want their child to succeed. I have never met a student who didn't want to learn.

This book invites you to come with me to the heart of the public education system. I am the observer who sits silently in the corner of the classroom. I am the interviewer who talks to students, teachers, families, and hears heartwarming and heart wrenching stories. I am the recorder, and reporter, and the messenger.

Whenever an education program is funded, its sponsors want to know if it works, how it works, and where it works. In search of answers to those questions, I have spent my career in inner-city and rural schools. Many Monday mornings I have stood in front of a new school, knowing nothing about it except that I am confident that I will leave three days later bearing many of its secrets. Every school district is a galaxy and every school a different planet.

For my work, I have been paid by various agencies of the federal government, state departments of education, and even local school districts. Occasionally, my client has been a philanthropic organization like the Kellogg Foundation and the Lilly Endowment.

Acknowledgments

Ira Shull, who died too young, was my first editor and mentor. His criticisms were gentle, his praise heartfelt, and his belief in me and my story are the reason that the book exists today. Thank you also to Fiona Hallowell for additional editing; and to Michael Wright, my agent; and Tom Koerner of Rowman & Littlefield who brought the book to fruition.

My writing benefitted immensely from editing and critiques from my friends, Susan Chayet and Dr. Kathleen Mackin, who read, reread, and suggested ways to improve the book without ever discouraging me. Finally, to my friends and colleagues. I had to change your names in the book, but you know who you are. Thank you for enriching my life and making the journey interesting and exciting.

Introduction

Books written by education researchers generally keep their distance from the gritty realities of the daily lives and experience of students and their families. Such expertise serves the needs of the research community and the academics who tend the knowledge base. Their contributions to education reform and innovation are immense, but their viewpoint is limited.

Like a journalist embedded with the troops at the front lines, the messages from the book are communiques that come from the edge of education, where the poorest students and their families struggle to find a path out of poverty through education.

It often does seem like a battlefield. The enemy is education agencies that are not always about education and schools that are not always about students. The enemy is teachers who don't care and a system that seems willing to write off some students and their families as disposable.

Ranged against the enemy are teachers who are inspired, caring, and successful with students who might have been written off, schools that understand that connectedness and belonging are the best antidotes to apathy and alienation, and families that advocate for their children.

It is a terrible irony that innovations and interventions either stop at the door of very poor schools or that, given an intervention, these schools do not have the skills to implement them successfully. It is sad that the parents who need to advocate most strongly for their children are the least likely to have the skills and knowledge to do so. The first best weapon against injustice is knowledge. You cannot right a wrong of which you are unaware. The purpose of this book is to provide that first best weapon.

The book has five sections. It begins with a section on students and their families, the place where as Yeats said, "all the ladders start."[1] The second section examines teachers and instruction, the voice of the education system that students hear every day. Some students are very fortunate; others are not.

Section 3 contains sad and somber revelations about the schools that most people would not want to visit, the schools in which teachers and students alike are punished with an extreme poverty of resources and an inability to provide students with hope, much less education. You would not want to send your children there, but parents who are as caring as you are face these schools every day.

The fourth section of the book moves outside the school to look at testing and evaluation. The obsession with standardized testing became a shameful interlude in American education and exposed the willingness of some in the establishment to ignore the welfare of students in order to magnify the successes they were not actually producing. The skills to conduct evaluations at the school or district levels are covered in a chapter dedicated to addressing the hard questions in helpful ways.

The conclusions of the book present a solution based on visions. Systemic thinking has brought change in education, but education is not about systems, it is about people. The message is not so much "Back to the drawing board" as "Throw away the drawing board and start with the students."

An appendix of tools provides simple, easy-to-use survey and interview protocols, so that administrators can test the waters before they jump in to investing in professional development or external intervention. An important set of tools concerns attitudes toward special education and the responses of families and teachers to the special education program in your school.

NOTE

1. W. B. Yeats, "The Circus Animals' Desertion," *W. B. Yeats Collected Poems* (London: Picador Press, 1995), 391.

Section One

STUDENTS AND FAMILIES

Chapter 1

How Students Experience School

Students are the customers of the education system, but their voices can scarcely be heard above the cacophony of adults speaking for them or about them: "What these kids need . . ."; "Kids today don't care . . ."; and "When I was in school . . ."

Students are not widgets moving along an assembly line; they have experiences to share, and opinions and questions to offer. Beyond an occasional focus group, student interview, or classroom observation, traditional program evaluations have not given much attention to the students either. This chapter contrasts traditional observation techniques with two innovative approaches to gathering data from the students' perspective.

TRADITIONAL CLASSROOM OBSERVATION

A traditional classroom observation takes about twenty to thirty minutes in an elementary school, or one class period in middle or high schools. Observers often carry a checklist of what particular practices or elements are the target of the observation. These classroom visits are a snapshot of the class without a larger context.

For example, the observer's notes might state that "students are working from a textbook." The observer has no way of knowing if the students were working from textbooks before they were observed and if they continue to work from textbooks all day long.

Also, in typical classroom observations, teachers know in advance when the visit to their classrooms will take place. Some prepare for the observation by scheduling an activity like a video or a writing assignment that involves little or no interactive instruction. In those cases, the teachers' purpose is apparently to show that the students are usefully occupied while not exposing themselves to criticism of their instructional skills.

LEARNING TO SEE INSTRUCTION FROM
THE STUDENTS' POINT OF VIEW

The opportunity to understand the delivery of instructional services from the students' perspective, through a process called Shadowing, was part of a national study of programmatic interventions in low income schools. Shadowing entailed following a single student through the entire school day, taking detailed notes on every class and every interaction that the Shadowed student experienced.

For the researchers who took part in that study, the process of Shadowing individual students was eye-opening. A conference presentation to the American Educational Research Association titled "Everywhere that Mary Went"[1] pretty much summed up the Shadowing experience. Students were not Shadowed to gym, lunch, or recess; otherwise, if you saw Mary, you saw her Shadow. The education researchers who took on Shadowing had conducted school visits and classroom observations many times before, but they found that everything looked different when they examined instruction from the student perspective. The researchers wrote vivid descriptions of the good, the bad, and the ugly that they observed as they sat through entire days of Shadowing students.

The Good. For a third-grade science lesson, the teacher brought in a lovely old clock. It began to chime melodiously and the students were captivated. You could hear a pin drop as they listened. The teacher opened the clock and talked about pendulums. The action of the pendulum fascinated the students. Their heads swiveled back and forth like spectators at a tennis match.

The teacher explained that groups of students are to make their own pendulum. She showed them the three elements of the experiment; line, bob, and pivot. Then she demonstrated how to make the pendulum. The teacher asked them to predict what will happen if the bob is heavier; will it swing faster or slower? By showing instead of telling, the teacher made this lesson vivid and memorable.

For a third-grade vocabulary lesson, the students were paired up to read vocabulary words written on the board. The words included were: *grumpy, rude, unpleasant, grouchy, growled,* and *complaining.* They were asked to respond to the words by thinking of people they know who reminded them of the vocabulary words. Students shared ways in which they could cheer up a friend who was feeling like one of these words. In this activity, the teacher gave the words meaning relevant to the students' own experience.

For a fifth-grade social studies lesson on the drug-prevention program called DARE, a police officer talked to the class and gave them tips to avoid situations where they might be tempted to take drugs. There were several role-playing exercises. There was also a group discussion about what happens on the street and the students seemed very knowledgeable about drug action. One boy volunteered in response to a comment that "yeah, that happens on my corner."

The teacher noted that the students were able to express their feelings and their fears, as well as their awareness of what is happening in their communities. This was a lesson that brought the students' life experience into the conversation rather than giving them a lecture.

The Bad. In a third-grade science lesson, the teacher took a large gray rock out of a paper bag and asked the students to name it. They called out all sorts of words like rock, granite, and stone. She would not accept any of their responses. Finally, she drew their attention to the markings on the rock and someone called out, "It is a fossil."

Once the word she wanted was called, the teacher passed out a wonderful collection of fossils. Unfortunately, she did not talk about what they were or how they were formed. The students looked at them eagerly but learned nothing about them.

Without any preparation or discussion of the students' knowledge about fossils, the teacher began to read a book about dinosaurs. Most students were not listening and were still examining the fossils one by one as they passed them from hand to hand. Then she asked students to name differences in the fossils found in the book. However, not everyone was able to see the pictures in her little book.

For a fifth-grade poetry lesson, the teacher told the students that some of them were still writing poems as paragraphs and directed their attention to a page in the language arts book dealing with poetry. The teacher said "If it is not a poem, you cannot put it on the board." She looked at one student and said "What makes it a poem?" She repeated this several times before he replied, "I don't know."

The teacher then said, "That's why you have to read page 269." A boy asked, "Does it have to rhyme?" The teacher ignored his question and then became angry with students who had put several sentences on the same line. One student insisted on reading her poem aloud to the teacher who refused to hear it because it was not written in poetry format on the paper. This teacher completely sacrificed the meaning of poetry by focusing only on how it looked on the page. She also ignored students' questions that, had she answered them, might have helped them do better.

The Ugly. In a fifth-grade health lesson, the teacher instructed the students to clear their desks except for their health textbook. The teacher then left the room and her aide became responsible for teaching the lesson. The topic was about school psychologists.

The aide read from the textbook and then posed questions from it. She also asked the students to read part of the book silently. The lesson had potential for an excellent discussion as it asked the students to talk about the problems they might have that would require the help of a counselor. The students had some great questions and answers to the textbook questions, but the aide just let them drop with no follow-up or interaction among the students.

For a fifth-grade composition lesson, the students were writing about their plans for the future. One student asked to read his story aloud. He had written that he would remember this teacher and come back to "blow up her house and shoot her with a nine." The teacher asked, "A nine-millimeter?" The student said yes; the teacher nodded and he continued reading. Nothing more was said about the incident. Not only did the teacher respond inappropriately, but she failed to take advantage of a teachable moment to discuss the danger of firearms with the students.

This study was a seminal experience for researchers, and Shadowing students became a dimension of many subsequent projects. Once you have explored the student experience from the ground, research projects seem incomplete without it.

SHADOWING IN MIDDLE SCHOOLS

The experience of Shadowing in middle school turned out to be quite different from Shadowing in elementary school, where there was one classroom and only one or two teachers. Middle school students, moving from class to class, showed how they display different sides of themselves to different teachers.

While most elementary-school students were delighted to be Shadowed—often begging, "Please, miss, can you follow me too?"—middle-school students were unpredictable in their reactions. Some were excited to tell all about their teachers. "She's nice but she's really hard," or "He gets mad all the time. Once he broke his pencil in half and threw a book against the wall." Other students remained aloof, staying a careful three steps ahead of their Shadow, never turning their heads to acknowledge that the Shadowing process was taking place.

The teachers of the Shadowed students also displayed a range of attitudes. Some had a lot to say about the student and asked questions about the Shadowing process. Others merely nodded in acknowledgment and showed no interest in the process.

In describing students, some teachers put them into pigeon holes; for example, the hard worker, the lazy student, the good kid, the typical adolescent, or the troublemaker. They would be astonished to learn that their lazy student came alive in other classes or that their troublemaker could become a student completely engaged in learning.

The Troublemaker. Learning that Anthony would be Shadowed, the fifth-grade science teacher, Ms. Ryder, rolled her eyes and said, "Lots of luck with that." Anthony, who was within earshot, glanced up quickly and then looked down at his desk.

The science assignment for the day was to go outdoors to measure a tree. Ms. Ryder assigned the students to groups of three but did not make it clear which member of the group was responsible for measuring, who was going to record the measurements, or who was going to draw a sketch of the tree.

Anthony became visibly tense and anxious, his bony shoulders hunched up, his body tight as a bowstring. He seemed apprehensive about the upcoming experience.

Once outdoors, confusion took hold. Which tree? Was it a specific tree or any tree? How high up should they measure? Squabbles broke out about who was going to measure. Anthony snatched the measuring tape from a little girl and began flicking it at other students in a really annoying way. Ms. Ryder was drawing a detailed sketch of a tree and ignored the mayhem.

After she herded the students back to the classroom, Ms. Ryder began a discussion of what the students had learned from the tree-measurement experience. Anthony waved his hand frantically to answer every question, but Ms. Ryder never looked his way or acknowledged him. Finally, he yelled out. "Call on me. You never have." She acted as if she didn't hear him. Nonetheless, as he was leaving the class, she handed him a detention slip.

The next class was math. It was right across the hall from the science classroom and as he entered the room, Anthony's face was still tightened into a mask of anger just barely contained. Fortunately, his math teacher saw his expression and reacted to it. Putting her arm around him, she suggested that Anthony work by himself at the computer for this class session. Sitting alone, wearing earphones, Anthony gradually relaxed and become absorbed in the screen in front of him.

The Lazy Student. David was a sixth-grader who one teacher described as "a kid who won't do a thing beyond the absolute minimum." David paid no attention to his Shadow and his habitual expression would have fit nicely in a mug shot. In his previous classes, David had done his work and responded to questions directed specifically to him, but otherwise seemed disengaged.

The last class of the day was science. The science classroom was a realm of controlled chaos. Students were sitting on the floor in various stages of covering cardboard cartons with aluminum foil. Their voices were loud and excited. The teacher was lying on the floor with his head in a cardboard box, helping to make an oven. He had written the objective of the project on the board. "The purpose of this experiment is to design a solar oven able to withstand a wind stability and a directionality test."

Within a few minutes in this class, David changed into a deeply engaged young scientist. Working with three other boys to construct their solar oven, he got into a disagreement about the effect of using too much foil.

One member of the group seemed determined to wrap the oven in every inch of the roll of foil they had been given. David thought too much foil would keep the oven from working correctly. Suddenly, David acknowledged his Shadow, asked her opinion on the foil issue, and became animated and downright chatty.

David explained that their goal was to place the ovens on the roof patio on a sunny day and bake brownies. However, before doing so, the ovens had to withstand the window fan turned to high for one minute without moving. He had great confidence in his group's oven design and even invited his Shadow back to eat some brownies. The David that the science teacher knew would not have been recognized by his other teachers.

The Typical Adolescent. Melissa was an eighth-grader who avoided contact with her Shadow by moving from class to class with a protective pod of giggling girlfriends. It was unclear if Melissa learned anything during the day because she spent most of her time drawing intricate hearts and flowers on the front of her notebook and writing surreptitious notes to her friends.

Melissa was a little late for social studies since the pod dawdled on the way. When she got to class, the teacher was moderating a discussion of Incan civilization using a detailed drawing of an Incan settlement displayed on the SMART Board. The teacher posed questions: "From this picture, what can you tell us about the location of this Incan settlement? What would be the pros and cons of having a settlement in such a location? Why would such a location be of benefit to the Inca?"

Students engaged in a spirited conversation as the teacher pointed out specific clues in the picture. Melissa came to life and for the first time that day; she volunteered to take part. She raised her hand and leaned forward in her chair. Her habitual sullen expression wiped away, Melissa became a beautifully engaged student, responding to the effect of a teacher awakening her intellect.

KIDS WITH CAMERAS

The experience of Shadowing led to a desire to see more intimate examples of the students' point of view and to better understand their school experience. Kids with Cameras was adapted from a tool developed by the National Park Service to measure the comparative attractiveness of sights within their parks.

The Park Service gave disposable cameras to tourists as they entered the park, asked them to take pictures of their favorite places, and then collected the cameras as the tourists left.

The adaptation that became Kids with Cameras was to distribute disposable cameras to students at the middle- or high-school level, asking them to take pictures of the things and people most important to them. Sometimes, the cameras were given to students who were also being Shadowed and sometimes to a mixed group, perhaps a combination of student council members and students with disabilities.

The only rule for using the cameras was that students could take no more than three pictures of their friends. Once the pictures were developed, individual interviews with the students were conducted, showing each photo and asking: "Why is this important to you?"

Manuel was a special education student in middle school. Manuel's family were migrant workers and he spoke very little English. School was a daily struggle for him. On his camera were several pictures of the butterfly garden, a point of pride for the school.

Manual said, "Sometimes, when school is too hard or people are mean to me, I go to the beautiful garden. It makes me feel better and if I am crying, no one is there to see me. The garden is my home."

The most important part of the Kids with Cameras endeavor was to convene interested adults to reflect on what the pictures communicated about the school, and how the school could create stronger connections with its students. As part of the process, the researchers often made PowerPoint presentations of the photos and comments to show to teachers and administrators.

The presentations invariably brought wonderment and sometimes tears. Manuel's comments about the pictures of the butterfly garden caused gasps among his teachers. One said, "I always thought he was such a happy, easygoing kid." Another teacher with tears in her eyes said, "I just want to go hug him right now."

Teachers were a favorite subject of Kids with Cameras. Surprisingly, they never photographed a teacher they didn't like, but the students took many pictures of teachers they did like. In the interviews, they said things like, "She really cares about us. She asks me how I am every day when I come to her class." "She showed us her engagement ring and invited all of us to the wedding." "He will stay after school any day, if you ask him for extra help."

Students seldom took pictures of the principal, usually a more remote figure in their lives, but at McKinley Middle School, the principal, Mr. Conti, appeared in every set of pictures. Mr. Conti created powerful connections with students. "He can make a bully cry," said one student. "You can be in trouble with him one day," said another, "but the next day, he's not mad anymore."

There were several images of Mr. Conti's neckties. Each morning a different student chose which of the many colorful ties displayed in the office Mr. Conti would wear that day. The students took tremendous pride in that small gesture. "He's wearing my tie today."

One student took a picture of the suggestion box, which had a prominent place in the hallway. "You can ask anything you want to and Mr. Conti will answer you, but you have to look at yourself when you put something in." He pointed to the mirror that hung directly over the box. "When you look in the mirror, you think about whether you are proud you made the comment, or maybe it's something you don't want to say."

Mary Lou, a deaf student with learning disabilities, took pictures that highlighted the importance of various specialists in her life such as the hearing specialist, her interpreters, and sign language teacher. There is also one of nondisabled friends sitting at a cafeteria table. When asked about the significance of that picture Mary Lou said, "They ask how my day is."

Mary Lou found an identity by becoming president of the American Sign Language Club in her high school. One of her pictures showed the group out to dinner at a local restaurant. For a group of profoundly deaf students, this public experience was a watershed moment.

Hannah, another special education student, who had seemed completely indifferent to classes all day, took a picture of the hot air balloon on the cover of her social studies textbook. She said it was about her dream that she would one day leave her neighborhood, "Fly far away and see the whole world." Looking at the picture and hearing Hannah's words, one of her teachers said, "I am humbled. I have always believed the only thought she had in her mind was boys, boys, boys."

Shadowing and Kids with Cameras have different but related purposes. The focus of Shadowing is on the interactions of teachers and students, teachers' perception of students, and the multidimensional experience of students in classrooms. Kids with Cameras is a way of capturing how students feel about school; it is absolutely personal and completely honest.

Researchers cannot stop the behavior of a harsh teacher or incompetent teacher, but they can at least document their crimes of commission and omission through Shadowing. Similarly, they cannot reward the beautiful experiences some teachers give their students, but they can document those too and hope that when they speak truth to power, power is listening.

Kids with Cameras is nowhere near as deep an examination of students' experiences as Shadowing, but it is immediate and satisfying. Teachers watch the PowerPoints of the pictures and stories told by students and they react. They sometimes say that they have heard something that will stay with them forever. For example, one student said about her picture, "This is Ms. Baker.

She's my English teacher. My goal in life is to be a teacher just like Ms. Baker."

Teachers hear their students say wonderful things about them and feel rewarded for the work they do and the efforts they make, which are often unseen by anyone other than the students in their classrooms. One teacher said, "It's like getting a teacher of the year award, only better."

What we learn from Shadowing and Kids with Cameras is that students are multidimensional and that some are difficult to motivate. Active learning, close relationships, and a recognition that children don't conform to stereotypes can make school a better learning experience for those students. Teachers who recognize and respond to the talents and learning styles of students will be rewarded by seeing their students improve academically and thrive emotionally.

IN YOUR TOOLBOX

A copy of the evaluation tools that support this chapter, *Shadowing* and *Kids with Cameras* appears in the appendix. The tools are also available for free per request to nbrighamassoc@yahoo.com.

NOTE

1. Nancy Brigham and Beth Gamse, "Everywhere That Mary Went: Looking at Students' Whole School Days," paper presentation, American Education Research Association, San Diego, 1993.

Chapter 2

Addressing School Violence through Student Connectedness

When a student or former student bursts into a school and begins indiscriminately killing students, teachers, administrators, and staff, his actions seem completely unfathomable. Yet the killer may be leaving important clues. He does not choose a random location or even a random school; he attacks a school he has attended.

Once he starts shooting, it usually doesn't matter who the victims are because he is not killing individuals, he is killing school, the place where he learned that he would never belong to the community of students and teachers.

School is more than a place to acquire skills in reading, writing, and arithmetic. School is where a child finds out that he connects to others beyond his own family, or he does not make connections.

As his peers learn to read, does he see jumbles of characters where they see words? Do other children want to play with him or does he find out that, for reasons he does not understand, he is called "weird" as if they know something about him that he has not yet recognized in himself? Do the teachers value him for who he is or does he feel invisible or ignored? Does he seek attention in negative ways because that is the only way he believes he will be noticed?

Students are likely to spend more of their waking hours with teachers than with their families. The teachers become role models and even surrogate parents as well as educators, and if some teachers say that's not what they signed up for, it is nevertheless true.

Young people who commit suicide and those who commit mass murder are driven by many of the same forces. One turns the violence inward; the other turns it outward and kills innocent victims. Some end up doing both, killing others and then themselves. Both the students who commit suicide and those who become killers are likely to have a history of being bullied and alienated from the school community by their peers and even by their teachers.

When teachers are asked if their school is a community for students, they look taken aback by the question, but the students always know. Given the opportunity, a student focus group will talk eagerly about connectedness. They understand the importance of relationships, traditions, extracurricular activities and sports, which comprise the connective web that supports them through their middle- and high-school years.

A study reported in *Educational Leadership* concluded that connectedness "refers to students' school experiences and their perceptions and feelings about school." This includes: "feeling that they are a part of the school; that adults at school care about them personally; that their learning matters and is a high priority; that they are close to people at school; have supportive relationships with adults; and, that teachers and staff consistently treat them with respect."[1]

Research also shows that a connection to school is critically important in keeping students in school and helping them to succeed academically. "Strong scientific evidence demonstrates that increased student connection to school promotes motivation, classroom engagement and improved school attendance. These three factors in turn increase academic achievement. These findings apply across racial, ethnic, and income groups."[2]

It is rare to find two schools that are perfect exemplars of an abstract concept such as connectedness, but Jaguar High School and another public school, Swansdown Academic Preparatory School, are archetypes. Jaguar connected with its students at many levels and the other school, Swansdown, rather deliberately, chose not to.

PHYSICAL AND EMOTIONAL SAFETY

The greatest current fear focuses on the extreme violence of school shootings, but students have felt afraid in school before the shootings became the national narrative. Sometimes, they are afraid of internal school violence inflicted on them by teachers and other students. One Swansdown eighth-grader said, "I just don't feel safe here sometimes. One teacher threw me up against the wall because she said I was being disrespectful." Another student added, "The teachers do not try to make us feel safe."

According to a survey that asked students and teachers many identical questions, the Swansdown teachers were actually less convinced than students about school safety. While 50 percent of students reported that the school was a safe place, just 31 percent of the teachers believed their students were safe at Swansdown.

Researchers identified Jaguar High School as part of a study that focused on schools that were successful in serving students with disabilities. As part of the research, the survey responses of students with disabilities were analyzed separately. In every area of belonging and connection, their responses were even more positive than those of the general education students.

For example, 92 percent of the students with disabilities reported that they felt safe in school and that their teachers cared about them. An alumnus of the special education program at Jaguar recalled, "We had all the best teachers, all the teachers who cared the most about students. I felt sorry for the general education students. I really did."

Identity and Traditions

"You don't go to Jaguar, you belong to it," a tenth-grade student said and the whole student focus group nodded in agreement. "Nothing holds this school together" an eleventh-grader at Swansdown said and the whole student focus group nodded in agreement.

Jaguar High School is an established school steeped in tradition. A student explained that being part of Jaguar sets students apart. She said that when Jaguar students talk to students who attend other schools, they often say, "You wouldn't understand, it's a Jaguar thing."

The word "tradition" is probably the single word most frequently used when people describe the school. Many families in the area are military or retired military and patriotism is another piece of the Jaguar tradition. It is this blend that caused a school board member to call Jaguar "the last real high school in America."

Swansdown is in the process of becoming a high school by adding a grade to the middle school each year. Swansdown's sole focus is academics, in particular a rigorous and challenging curriculum that will prepare every student for college. Most parents of Swansdown students did not attend college and the school has a high concentration of minority and economically disadvantaged students.

Many students believe that the school's designation as a "preparatory school" was the major reason their families chose Swansdown. A student said: "My mom heard the word 'preparatory' and she was sold!"

The Swansdown students sensed that their school needed to create a separate identity. "It's not really a high school. We don't even have all our classes separate from the middle-school kids. If we got this far we should be singled out. The middle-school kids have their chance to go to high school later."

Several were angry that their high-school orientation was paltry compared to other high schools in the city. "Welcome to high school. Now go home . . .

we had a thirty-minute pep rally; the other high school had a whole day! They got balloons and we didn't."

Teacher Attitudes

The Swansdown teachers said. "There is camaraderie among teachers. We are very supportive of each other." But a focus group of students said the teachers were not supportive of the students. Like many schools, Swansdown has become a comfortable community of adults but the community does not extend to the students.

One Swansdown eighth-grade student in a focus group turned bright red as he introduced himself and said, "One thing I want to say is, that I really want you to know, is that the teachers are evil. The food is bad, the administration doesn't know what it's doing, and the teachers don't know the kids."

Another added, "This school is unsafe, disorganized, and unfair! There aren't any adults in this school you can trust."

At Swansdown, the gap between the teachers' view of their relationship with students and the students' view was startling. Several questions on the survey explored dimensions of community. One question was, "How many students feel they belong in this school?" At Jaguar, 96 percent of students gave positive responses; at Swansdown it was 64 percent.

At Jaguar, 87 percent of the students and about the same number of teachers reported that when they woke up in the morning, they looked forward to coming to school. Swansdown teachers also looked forward to going to school every day, but the majority of students did not.

This type of response has been the case in other schools but never before have the numbers been so skewed. At Swansdown, 93 percent of the teachers and 13 percent of the students said that they look forward to coming to school, an 80 percent difference.

Another telling disparity between Swansdown teachers and students was their reply to the survey item "Students believe school work is important." On the survey, 87 percent of students agreed that yes, school work was important. Of the teachers, only 28 percent responded that they thought school work was important to their students. One teacher in a focus group said, "In one of my classes of twenty-five students, about one-quarter of the class are late, unprepared, and refuse to do the work. It's a social gathering."

Administrators apparently believed that wearing uniforms would create an identity for students at Swansdown. The principal said that the purpose of the uniform was to instill pride and responsibility in their students and that it was important to achieve that goal.

The school secretary was in charge of enforcing the school uniform law and she tackled her job forcefully. As visitors entered the school office, they were greeted by the sight of an eighth-grader standing stiffly as the secretary leaned over the high counter to berate him.

"This is your second infraction. One more and you will be sent home for the day and I will have to notify your parents. You know you get two shirts at the beginning of the year. You are supposed to wear one and wash the other one. You know that, don't you?"

When the student mumbled something about both shirts being dirty, she leaned toward him over the counter and said loudly: "I won't accept that excuse. It's up to you to do your own laundry and make sure you have a clean shirt every day."

Jaguar High School students did not wear uniforms but they did follow a dress code, which was put in place by a community committee comprised of alumni. One member of that committee said, "This summer we had a safety committee. We actually rewrote the dress code. I walk in here now and I see kids and I'm like, it's working, it's working."

Competition

Competition both in sports and academics is very important to Jaguar and to the local community. One of the alumni told a story about his football experience.

"When I was a sophomore, we made it to the state championship football game, but we lost 10 to 7. When we rolled into town, probably at one o'clock in the morning, there was a gym full of five thousand people cheering us. What I learned from that experience is that how you play, how you work, and the attitude that you bring to it is important. I have remembered that all my life."

The education director from the local cable television station came to talk about their annual Academic Tournament. She said that nearby Peaceville was the academic powerhouse, looking to retire the trophy until they met up with Jaguar.

"Everybody was positive Peaceville was about to win their second trophy. Then, Jaguar came out of the starting gate and just whipped the socks off of them and it was unbelievable to watch. I'm always impressed by Jaguar's demeanor. They come into the studio in their blue shirts and they come to play."

Competition, other than academic competition, is not part of the Swansdown ethos. A teacher noted, "The students have no extracurricular activities except sports and right now there's a problem with the gym floor, so now they don't even have sports. I don't think fixing the floor is a priority."

Extracurricular Activities

Extracurricular clubs and activities are an integral part of the Jaguar land-scape. Any group of students can start a club if they find a faculty sponsor. On the sign-up sheets posted near the main office, the names of twenty-seven different clubs were listed, each with a credible number of members.

One activity was the Minority Council founded by a Jaguar guidance counselor, who is also a Jaguar graduate. During her time in high school, this counselor was the first African American to become a cheerleader. In doing this she faced criticism from both sides. The white students more or less ignored her while the African American students criticized her for doing "a white thing."

When she became a counselor, she helped Jaguar students to form the Minority Council to ensure that they had a voice in the school. The Minority Council had a large membership and one mother said, "It knocked the chip off my daughter's shoulder and now she feels proud of who she is."

At Swansdown, students are also allowed to form clubs if they can find a sponsor. According to the students, none of the teachers want to be a sponsor. One teacher acknowledged there were not enough opportunities for kids. "There's no newspaper, no yearbook, no prom either."

A student said, "The teachers say that students need to take charge and create clubs and activities, but we need some help. Have you seen the teachers run out of here as soon as school ends? They don't want to stay and do things with us. They just want to go home. We have nothing to be proud of, nothing to put on our college applications."

Swansdown does have a band and it was the one thing every student focus group spoke about enthusiastically. It was not clear if it was the band or the band teacher they loved. "The band teacher is great. If he was the face of this school it would be a great school. If you see him in the hall he says, 'Isn't this a great school?'"

Family and Community Involvement

The gap between students' and teachers' perceptions at Swansdown is distressing. While only 42 percent of the students responded that the school encourages family involvement, 92 percent of the teachers believe that family involvement was encouraged. It is unlikely that the teachers will make any effort to improve the school's relationship with families if the teachers are happy with what they believe is the status quo. They also don't know the students' perceptions and would probably be surprised.

A teacher who is a relative newcomer to the faculty at Jaguar reported, "Everyone seems to have a piece of this school. There's like thirty or forty alumni who teach here. They come back. I'm not an alumni, but I'm a president of another club. I'm the president of the *Alum-nots*. Funky things like that happen around here and it's all for fun. I'm not lying to you when I say it's just a family and everyone counts."

Alienation

Alienation from school is a feeling of being left out of things in which you believe you should be included, as well as a sense that no one is listening to you. Alienation is often associated with large schools. Swansdown is a very small school, so why do so many Swansdown students feel unheard and unappreciated?

In the survey, 38 percent of students said "teachers don't know me very well." Only 13 percent said they would go to a teacher if they had a problem and only 5 percent said that teachers appreciated students' contributions to the school.

At Jaguar, a student who knew all about alienation was excited to talk about it. Jared had only one desire in life, which was to join the military. Before he came to Jaguar, a counselor at his middle school told Jared that because of his learning disability he was not smart enough to join the military and would be "lucky" if he even graduated from high school.

In middle school, he was placed in segregated special-education classes for math and reading. Jared started to act out and to get in trouble in school. At home, he was so withdrawn that his parents feared he would attempt suicide. He admitted that he had thought about it.

As soon as he attended Jaguar, Jared's transformation became a convergence of changes both in academics and in his social environment. The opportunity to participate in ROTC was transformative for Jared. It is notable that Jaguar had many students with disabilities, male and female, enrolled in ROTC. One teacher said the students liked the structure of the drills and the feeling of importance that wearing a uniform gave them. "It is a place for them to succeed."

For Jared, it was the proudest accomplishment of his life. He said: "They teach us here what we are going to do if we join the real military. Like today we'll go outside and march. Ordinary kids just sit down when they enter a classroom, but we don't do that. We have to stand up until we are called to attention and then we get to sit down."

In tenth grade, Jared's test scores in both reading and math were at the fifth-grade level. The special education staff helped him to understand his learning disability and to participate in all general education classes. He explained to the researchers what his problem was and how he dealt with it.

"It's just real hard for me to focus and pay attention, really. There's not a day that goes by that I don't ask my teachers to explain something. . . . Yeah, I'm always really out there. . . . Yeah. Sometimes it takes the teacher a couple times to explain it to me. Maybe two or three times before I get it right."

Once he started to attend Jaguar, Jared became very advanced socially. In fact, Jared was one of two sophomore boys selected by his peers to be a member of the homecoming court, an honor he appreciated.

"I was picked from the sophomore class so I mean that is an honor to me actually, out of I don't know how many sophomores we have, but that's a lot of sophomores, so I guess they think very highly of me or something if I got chosen by them."

In his writing class, Jared chose to respond to the prompt "follow your dream." He explained to the class, "The reason I chose that one is because back in middle school, I was pretty much told that I wasn't smart enough to be in the military. I wasn't even smart enough to go on to graduate. I took that one to read because I can kind of rub it in their face now. I had to block that out of my head and say 'No. she's wrong. I can do it.'"

Jared was brought back from the brink of alienation, disengagement, and possibly self-harm by finding a place to belong, connections to his peers, and his first experience of academic success. These were the hallmarks of the Jaguar approach. To understand the importance of connections, you need only to think of how Jared would have turned out, the adult he could have become, if his life had continued as it was in middle school.

HARD AND SOFT SCHOOLS

A call for harder schools is a popular current reaction to school violence. A hard school is one that has more armed guards, fewer entrances, and gives weapons to teachers. The proponents of this approach seem to want to turn schools into fortresses.

However, a group of experts in school violence[3] say that the country would be better served by soft schools, which are defined by school climate. Climate is primarily defined by the quality of relationships among the students and the adults in a school.

Climate is also affected by the school's approach to discipline and behavior, the availability of professionals like counselors and social workers, as well as any social-emotional curriculum taught in the classroom. School climate, in turn, affects students' mental and emotional health and academic success. And research consistently finds key factors that can make schools safer: cultivate social and emotional health, and connect to community.

These experts go on to say, "No matter what you try to do by just hardening the target, we've learned that having the armed officers isn't necessarily going to stop it. Having the metal detector or the locked doors isn't going to stop it. The hard work is a lot more effort. You'd better start thinking in a more comprehensive manner about prevention instead of reacting."

NOTES

1. Robert Blum, "A Case for School Connectedness," *Educational Leadership* 62, no. 7 (April 2005): 6.

2. D. Wilson and D. Elliott, "The Interface of School Climate and School Connectedness: An Exploratory Review and Study," paper presentation, Wingspread Conference on School Connectedness: Strengthening Health and Educational Outcomes for Teens, Racine, WI, June 2003.

3. Anna Kamenetz, "Here's How to Prevent the Next School Shooting, Experts Say," NPR, https//www.npr.org/sections/ed2018/3/07/59087717. (Accessed June 12, 2018.)

Chapter 3

Jeremy: A Boy on a Tightrope

Shadowing individual students is different from conducting other student observations. The researcher spends one-on-one time following the student from class to class over a period of several days, perhaps even over the course of three years. Shadowing includes interviews with the students, their teachers, and their parents. The researcher talks informally with the students and watches them struggle or shine in various situations. Inevitably the students draw the observers into their stories.

Shadowing Jeremy was an experience that sometimes became alarming. Many people thought that they knew him, but no one seemed to hear or see the struggles that went on in his mind every day. His story is more than a case of a student falling through the cracks of the system. It is a saga of multiple betrayals by all the people that were supposed to care about him.

When you think about school violence, you wonder how many students like Jeremy are desperate for help but are not asking for it, how many come to the conclusion that there is no one in the adult world they can trust. Jeremy, during the three years he was Shadowed, remained a boy on a tight rope, just barely suspended above the abyss of drugs and chaos.

Drake Middle School, which Jeremy attended, was involved in a study of middle schools that formed meaningful relationships with families of students with disabilities. Jeremy was a member of a student focus group; the research was conducted on the first day of the school visit. The focus group included four special education students and four students from the school's gifted-and-talented program. The theme of the focus group was how students felt about the school.

Jeremy sat next to Seth, a child beset with so many tics and unusual physical mannerisms that it was painful to watch him talk. Although the other students looked down at the table in embarrassment while Seth attempted to communicate, Jeremy smiled and nodded at him and even provided words here and there when Seth struggled to find them.

Jeremy was the glue that held the group together, always quick to say, "That's right!" or "I think so too." Having assumed he was one of the gifted students, it was a surprise for the researcher to learn that he was in fact a special education student, one of those who would be Shadowed.

The school social worker, Alicia, had nominated the school for inclusion in the study and also chosen the students to Shadow. She picked students whose families she counseled because they were struggling at home and looking to the school for support. As a result, the students selected at Drake Middle School came from families that were far from typical and often in crisis.

Alicia apologized that Jeremy's parents would not be available for interviews because they were both in federal prison for transporting drugs from Mexico into the United States with intent to sell. Alicia expected Jeremy's mom to be released by the time of the first school visit, but some bureaucratic snafu had pushed back her release date and she continued to live in a halfway house.

With the freedom to make phone calls, which she had not enjoyed while in prison, Charlotte, Jeremy's mom, called the school frequently from the halfway house and Alicia said she was "pretty involved with Jeremy." She added that Charlotte would be released in time for a parent interview the following spring.

The folder of information on Jeremy's history was longer than average and full of mysteries and surprises. His first special-education diagnosis in elementary school was "emotional disturbance." There were documented instances of Jeremy fighting and throwing items on the floor or at other students. Surprisingly though, the diagnosis at the middle school was changed from "emotional disturbance" to "information processing difficulties."

Despite his diagnosis, Jeremy had no contact with the special education department. The only service he received was weekly therapy sessions with Alicia. The school's special education director said that she knew very little about Jeremy and had never dealt with him directly. If Jeremy had difficulty processing information, it seemed odd that he was not given any instructional support, but that was one of several mysteries about Jeremy's life in and out of school.

At fourteen, Jeremy looked more like a short, stocky man than a young adolescent. His features seemed older than his age; he had very broad shoulders and a man's deep voice.

On the first morning of Shadowing, Jeremy was waiting for the researchers at the school's main office. He was concerned that the observer would not know where to find him, since he spent his first school period as a coach in a physical education program for students with severe mental and physical disabilities. "It's not on my schedule," he said. "It's a volunteer thing I do. I'm a special education student and they are too, so I feel like I should be with them."

Jeremy's student was Henry, a boy with severe mental and emotional handicaps. The first activity in the gym found them all sitting on the floor in a big circle; coaches, athletes, teachers, and aides. They did arm and leg exercises. Henry did not seem to need much help, and Jeremy did not interact with him except to nod approvingly each time Henry got into the right position.

Dancing to a CD that was mostly about body parts (raise your hands, flap your arms) was lively and all the students, coaches, and teachers seemed quite engaged with it. Each coach and teacher danced with a student with a disability.

For the first time, Jeremy took the initiative with Henry. "Hey buddy, come over and stand by me. We're going to dance." He danced Henry away from the group, so they were dancing alone in a corner of the gym. Later Jeremy explained that he could sense that Henry was about to get upset and he knew why.

He said, "Henry has imaginary enemies and they get him upset. He can really lose it. He believes that another student, Tony, is one of his enemies. Unfortunately, Tony looks up to Henry and always wants to be near him." Jeremy had seen Tony moving toward Henry and wanted to move Henry away before he lost control.

The coaches escorted the students back to class and then waited in a corner of their classroom for the end of the class period. Jeremy seemed a little anxious and when the teacher came in; he immediately buttonholed her to say, "I think you wanted to give them the Special Olympics handout today." The teacher nodded and went to get the handouts. Another student coach exclaimed, "Jeremy, what would we do without you?" Her tone was admiring, not sarcastic.

Jeremy's first academic class was English, and when he neared the door, he said matter-of-factly, "I may be in trouble here. I was out for six days with pneumonia and I have to make up a lot of work." The teacher's curt greeting, however, was: "Late again, Jeremy!"

The teacher did not know about Jeremy's volunteer coaching and when the observer mentioned his activities she said, "If you told me, Jeremy, I would understand why you are often late. That's a wonderful thing you are doing." Jeremy did not accept the compliment well; his reaction was to turn bright red and duck his head in embarrassment.

Later, the teacher did remind Jeremy that he had homework to catch up on and suggested he come after school that day and get a start on it. Jeremy just nodded, but later said that he was planning to go to science class to make up work after school, not English class.

Why had he not told the English teacher the truth about his plan? Throughout the first three days he was Shadowed, all his teachers were on his case about work he had missed while he was absent with pneumonia.

Rather than going to the teachers to discuss a schedule, Jeremy decided how and in what order he would make up the work. He was sticking to his own schedule without advising any of his teachers either that he had work in other classes to make up or what his plan was for getting it done. He confided later that he had concluded that he needed to be independent and self-directed, which made it hard for him to take advice or guidance from teachers or other adults.

None of his six teachers knew anything about Jeremy except what he presented in class. Not one of them knew he was a special education student, nor had they read his Individualized Education Plan (IEP). They characterized Jeremy as "smart but disorganized" or "lazy" or "undisciplined." Observing him, that was not the image he portrayed.

In each class, he would clear his desk of everything except what he was working on, put his head down, and focus. He could have been an A student but he was getting B's and C's. Homework was his downfall. He forgot to take it home, forgot to do it, forgot to bring it back to school, or he brought it with him and forgot to hand it in. All his teachers were disturbed about his missing homework and taking points off his grades. He told them he would improve but he didn't.

Enclosed in the folder of information about Jeremy, the researcher found the first chapter of a book that Jeremy was writing about his life, with Alicia's encouragement. The chapter in the folder was called "No Fingers Lost," and recounted his memories of the time two men broke into his parents' house because his mother owed them money for drugs.

In the story, Jeremy, who was in kindergarten at the time of the incident, called the men "Blubber" and "Twig." Twig was the thin one carrying a knife and Blubber was the fat one with a gun. Blubber took the three children upstairs and put a gun to Jeremy's head. Twig stayed downstairs with Jeremy's mom.

Jeremy wrote, "I was more scared than jumping over a three-foot-wide snake pit. I thought I was going to be shot." Meanwhile, the children heard their mother screaming and pleading with Twig, "Don't cut off my fingers. I just don't have the money now. I will get it for you later." A neighbor, hearing the ruckus, called 911 and when Blubber and Twig heard approaching police sirens, they ran away grabbing the TV and VCR as they left.

Jeremy managed to find a positive ending for this horrendous event. The men were apprehended, the TV and VCR were recovered, and the two men were sentenced to forty-three years in prison. "I am glad I will never have to ever deal with them again," Jeremy wrote. He described himself as a person who "stays positive and tries to look at the bright side." He wrote that he always told his friends, "Look at me now. It's like it never happened."

A timeline of Jeremy's life provided a likely explanation of why he started acting out in school. During his early childhood, Jeremy's parents apparently took and sold drugs. He was starting second grade when both his parents were sent to jail for the first time, and he and his siblings spent one year in foster homes. At that time, Jeremy began to have outbursts in school and was given a special education label.

When his parents were released from jail and had their children back, they swore to them that they would never again get involved with drugs and, according to Jeremy, begged their children to trust them. His description of the years after that was, "So we got back together for two years and they did it again and we got taken away for one year. That time we were together for two years and then they were sent away again for four years and me and my brother ended up living with my Aunt Judy."

According to Alicia, Aunt Judy, an elderly woman who was actually Jeremy's great aunt, was a figure out of a Dickens novel. A special education teacher in the district, she was very strict with Jeremy and his brother and made them do many chores every day. Jeremy believed that the chores were excessive because his aunt believed that, left to his own devices, he would get into trouble.

Aunt Judy was religious and the boys spent a lot of time in church with her. They also had to write out a Bible verse every night before they went to bed. If she was not pleased with their behavior, they had to copy two verses.

Neither Aunt Judy nor Jeremy's dad, who was in a halfway house, became involved in the study, but in the spring Jeremy's mother, Charlotte, came to the school for an interview. Charlotte came into the room out of breath and grumpy. She said that if she had known the interview would take place on the second floor, she would not have come.

Her first question was if the $25 stipend offered to parents was in the form of cash or something else. She didn't like the something else, which was a gift certificate for a local grocery store chain. "There isn't one of those anywhere near where I live," she commented.

Charlotte began the interview by saying, "Jeremy isn't my smart one. Donnie, his younger brother, is my star. His teachers love him. You really should be studying Donnie." She wanted to talk more about Donnie but was convinced to tell a little about Jeremy's early childhood.

She said, "I honestly don't remember. I think Jeremy was a pretty responsible kid, but I couldn't really tell you. I was high all the time. Jeremy is my worrywart. I do remember one time when Tommy, Jeremy's dad, and I were worrying about how we were going to make the rent that month. Jeremy heard us and got all upset and offered to sell his bicycle to help out. It wasn't such a big deal. We had trouble coming up with the rent a lot of times."

Shifting in her chair to point at the tape recorder, Charlotte said firmly, "You can't believe everything that Jeremy has been writing and telling people. He's got a lot of it wrong."

The two thugs she said, had made a mistake; they came to the wrong house and threatened the wrong woman. According to her, the children and even her fingers were never in real danger. No one called 911. The police responding to another call in the neighborhood heard her screaming and "turned up on their own." And the guys were sentenced to thirty-four years, not forty-three years.

Having missed the significance of this incident to her children, she went on to miss the point of her betrayal of the children's trust. "No matter where I was," she said, "I called the boys every Sunday, even if I had to wait in line for the phone for an hour."

"I always called. I took a class and learned to crochet. They got presents from me all the time. They could rely on me. The kids know they can trust me," she said. "Jeremy knows that. I don't know why he is writing all this stuff and letting people read it."

It was a surprise to the interviewers that his mother had read Jeremy's book. Perhaps he had showed it to her to share his feelings. If so, it had no impact on her. Charlotte maintained an attitude of belligerent denial throughout the interview. It hadn't all happened and, if it did, it wasn't important.

It was fortunate that Charlotte was the last scheduled interview of the day since it spilled forty minutes over the one-hour time slot. In addition to being garrulous, she kept adding new information about the family.

Charlotte also now lived with Aunt Judy, although she hoped that would be temporary. Jeremy's dad, who was about to be released from prison, would live there soon. Grandma, who had lived with Aunt Judy even before the boys moved in, was a new character in the story since neither Alicia nor Jeremy had mentioned her.

Charlotte described grandma as "senile" and said she gave the boys conflicting orders and became incensed when they were not carried out. Also, until recently, Laura, Charlotte's oldest child from another relationship, and her two children had also lived in the house.

Laura had gotten heavily into drugs and Aunt Judy asked her to move out. While Laura's children, ages one and two, were living at Aunt Judy's, Jeremy was their primary babysitter. "He loves kids," Charlotte said.

Jeremy had said that he had too many chores. Charlotte said that one of the chores was to clean up after Aunt Judy's four dogs, who were not well trained and used the back porch as a bathroom. "The kids had to clean that up on their hands and knees," Charlotte reported.

No wonder Jeremy didn't get his homework done. Counting Laura and her two toddlers, eight people and four dogs had been living at Aunt Judy's house. In the midst of it, there was Jeremy taking care of the two toddlers, trying to figure out what Grandma wanted, and cleaning up after the dogs. He had no time to think, no time to himself. No wonder he became forgetful about his homework.

It became evident that Charlotte had come to the meeting with one major concern. Toward the end of the interview she stated, "That social worker, Alicia, is too involved with him. She has to learn that I'm his mother and I'm in charge of him now."

On that subject, Charlotte's concerns seemed valid. Why had Alicia not told his teachers that Jeremy had a special education designation? Why didn't she help him get some consideration concerning his homework? Why had she not referred him for psychological counseling outside the school? Why was she so proprietary of him? If he was a special education student, why didn't he have any contact with the special education department? The researcher was never able to get anyone to answer these questions.

The interview with Charlotte happened in May. The next visit to Drake Middle School was in October. A conversation with Alicia on the first day of the visit revealed that Jeremy's relationship with her had crashed and burned. She said, "Last year I kind of felt like the surrogate parent with him, like I was his mother at school. There were days that I would just lose it with him. I would say, 'You know, Jeremy, we had this conversation yesterday, what did you not understand about what we talked about?'"

Alicia now said that Jeremy had manipulated her. About the homework issue, she said, "He's a big boy." She reported that she told him, "It's time you stand on your own two feet and begin solving your own problems. You know you make decisions on your own. These are your choices."

She no longer met with him and Jeremy said, "She's calling us at home all the time to talk about my problems. I think she's trying to get me in trouble. I trusted her a lot last year, but now I guess I just feel she bugs me."

There was a struggle between Charlotte and Alicia about where Jeremy would go to school. In her interview, Charlotte said, "I want to take Jeremy out of this school and put him in a very good vocational school that's near where we're going to live."

Alicia had mentioned this conflict the previous spring. She believed Jeremy belonged in the Drake Middle School gifted program. She wanted his parents to give their permission for him to take the application test. His mother would not acknowledge that Jeremy belonged in the program. Charlotte said, "We hear that our younger son, Donnie, belongs in a gifted program but we never heard that about Jeremy."

In the fall, Jeremy was still at Drake Middle School, fighting with his parents about going to vocational school, and traveling an hour each way on the city bus from their new home to get to school. "I like it here. I like to play with my friends after school." "Play" was not a word you associated with Jeremy, but there he was after school, passing a football and running and tackling with several boys. It was strange to see Jeremy just being a kid.

The battle over vocational school continued and Charlotte was persistent. The school had refused Jeremy admission in February because they had already accepted their quota of students with disabilities. Charlotte went to the school district and got Jeremy's designation reversed. It is difficult to understand why Jeremy's special education label was so fungible. Was he emotionally disturbed, did he have difficulty processing information, or was he just fine?

Without formal special education meetings and tests, Jeremy's diagnosis changed from "emotional disturbance" to "information processing difficulties" and then disappeared entirely. That's not the way the system works. It may be that with her position in special education in the district, Aunt Judy did some behind-the-scenes manipulation. Now that Jeremy was not a special education student, the vocational school decided to accept him in April.

Jeremy did start his new school the same month of the research team's last visit to Drake Middle School. Charlotte agreed to meet them at a restaurant on the highway and let Jeremy go through his photos from Kids with Cameras. Jeremy's pictures were disappointing. He had no pictures of teachers or friends. There was a photo of the front of his new school and one taken inside an empty classroom.

Jeremy was not forthcoming about life at home or at school but talked a little about his ambitions. He had always wanted to be a fireman, but was now considering college and, "Maybe being a counselor because I'm good at that."

On the issue of trust, Jeremy said, "I cannot trust adults. I have to respect their authority but I have to rely on myself a lot of the time. I've just learned that for me, that's what works best."

Even a researcher sometimes feels the need to intervene. She asked, "But don't you see that sometimes you're substituting your judgment for an adult judgment that might be more informed or helpful for you?" "I do listen" he said, "unless it's something that shouldn't be done to me." And that's where the conversation ended.

Jeremy had brought an essay with him to the restaurant and shared its contents. The essay was called "Confusion." He may have intended it for inclusion in his book.

The essay started, "I am also a little confused about how my parents are doing. They told us that they wouldn't do drugs after the first time they were arrested. Then they promised they wouldn't even think about doing drugs again, but they did. I am beginning to open my heart and let them in again. If they break my heart again, I won't ever be able to trust them for the rest of my life. Then, where will I go and who will take care of me?"

The essay sounded as if he were asking for help, but he was unwilling to accept advice from the researcher, just as he had refused the advice of other adults. Jeremy was arrested the following summer. A passing policeman looked up and saw him sitting with his girlfriend on the roof of a building, dangling his feet over the edge and smoking marijuana.

It is easy to put all of the blame on Jeremy's parents for his predicament, but some blame must also accrue to Alicia, the social worker who kept Jeremy to herself. She confused her role as therapist with that of surrogate mother. She failed to refer Jeremy for outside professional counseling. She encouraged an exclusive relationship with him and then dropped him suddenly and cruelly.

His book and his essay were a cry for help, but neither his mother nor his social worker perceived them as such. Students like Jeremy are the most challenging to identify and help, but also the most critical if each young life matters. His fine mind, his compassion for others, and his sensitivity to the world around him were all balanced on that tightrope with him and he could not reach for a helping hand, even if one were extended to him.

Chapter 4

Family Connections

How Important?

If you spend enough time interviewing school administrators and teachers, you realize that many of them don't really want families involved as much as they say they do. Families are traditionally welcome only on the periphery of education; such as decorating for the holidays, holding bake sales, or chaperoning field trips. They are much less free to take part in making school policy or helping to plan their children's instruction.

Evaluations of federally funded national programs often require interviews with family and community representatives. The questions invariably concern the extent to which families are involved in the education of their children in meaningful ways, and whether the school has permeable boundaries to encourage connections with the community.

When the need arises for family members or community representatives to show up for interviews with researchers, many schools face a quandary. How can they demonstrate the school's close connection to families and the community when the relationship doesn't actually exist?

Savvy schools bring in staff from the local Chamber of Commerce as community representatives. Optimism is apparently a job requirement for working at the Chamber. The school administrators can be confident that the interview will affirm that this school is a great asset to the community.

Family members are more difficult to round up for interviews, but some schools have also found a way around that. The question that reveals this little bit of trickery is, "Do you have children in the school currently?" Often, the family members presented for interviews were employed as cafeteria workers, bus drivers, or classroom aides. Their children attended the school many years ago. These family members can be depended upon to speak highly of the school's relationship with families.

Parent organization members selected by the school for interviews were also reliably positive. They were willing to laminate identification badges for school staff, to make cookies for the bake sale, and to attend the spring musical even if their own child did not have a starring role. They supported the school; they didn't challenge it, even when the school needed to be challenged.

When they know an injustice has been done to their children, families may not intervene because they fear reprisals from the school. In a focus group of families whose children all attended the same high school, a mother remarked that her son recently had a bad experience. He had been placed in an Advanced Placement (AP) program in math for his upcoming junior year, but when school started, he was placed "down" in the regular math class.

Had he lost his math skills over the summer? He had not, and his mother called the school to find out the reason for his demotion. "They told me that the school did not have enough AP textbooks, so they had to limit the number of students to match the number of books. Your child was chosen at random to be deselected." Another mother added, "That happened to my daughter last year; she was so depressed."

These mothers were justifiably upset and angry, but they had done nothing to remedy the situation. Hearing this, other members of the focus group became outraged on their behalf and proffered solutions, such as going over the head of the principal to the superintendent, talking to the local newspaper, writing to the state superintendent.

Then, the mother of a student who had been removed from the AP program said, "If I do that, they will take it out on my daughter at school. I'm afraid she will pay for it if I get out of bounds," Apparently, the other parents resonated to this threat, because suddenly the wind went out of the sails of their rebellion.

FAMILIES OF STUDENTS WITH DISABILITIES

The one group of families required to do more than laminate, decorate, and bake are those who have children enrolled in special education. Federal legislation compels these families to enter into a formal, often uneasy, and sometimes confrontational relationship with the schools their children attend.

The federal law requires each student with a diagnosed disability to have an IEP signed as a legal agreement between the school and the family. The plan specifies exactly what accommodations will be provided to the student, such as how and where the student will receive instruction.

Public schools are required to serve a wide variety of students with dis-abilities, including students with mental illness, students with severe physical disabilities, and students from the full range of the autism spectrum. Federal law requires that all these students be educated in the "least restrictive environment."

The extent to which students with disabilities are educated apart from the general population of students is often a sore point between families and schools. The families almost always advocate for more inclusion in general education classes, while the school argues for separate settings, which they consider more appropriate and also makes it easier to schedule and provide instruction.

To comply with the letter of the federal law concerning the least restrictive environment, schools may practice "pretend inclusion." They place a large number of students with disabilities in a so-called general education class with a sprinkling of students without disabilities who are placed in the class to show that it is not a restrictive environment. "Inclusion kids" are actually still in the same situation they were before, that is separate from the mainstream of general education except for those four or five nondisabled students chosen for some reason to join them.

Research into the relationship between families and schools shows how complex and multifaceted it is. Even a research team with a background in special education made faulty, bad assumptions when they embarked upon a national search for middle schools that demonstrated true partnerships with families.

Four of these assumptions became apparent during the course of that research and caused some major midcourse corrections in the data-collection process. The four assumptions were: the importance of the IEP meeting; the definition of marginalized families; social isolation; and the importance of the IEP in classroom instruction.

The research team asked schools applying to be part of the study to complete a form stating how they made IEP meetings accessible to families. The language of the form was based on the researchers' assumption that the IEP meeting was the nucleus of the relationship between schools and families. It stated that the search focused on families who, "by reason of economic circumstances, educational attainment, cultural/linguistic differences, and/or minority status," were unlikely to take a proactive part in the IEP planning process.

Schools sent in interesting responses on their applications. For example, some said they held IEP meetings in a family's home or met with families at a neutral location, such as a local restaurant. One application, however, stated that the IEP meeting was just a date on the calendar for them because families of students with disabilities were included and welcomed all year long.

This information changed the selection process immediately. Why look for schools that hold one comfortable meeting a year when true partnership is one that integrates families into the process continuously?

MARGINALIZED FAMILIES

One component of the study was to select six traditionally marginalized families at each school to follow over time. The application defined marginalized families as those that might be prevented from participating fully in the IEP process because of "race, language, or other cultural differences." The wording of the application was the researchers' second faulty assumption.

Families can be marginalized in other, less obvious ways and their isolation is not confined to the IEP process, but more broadly from the school community. One of the selected families was marginalized because of mental illness, another was a family in which both parents were incarcerated.

The severity of their children's disabilities may also isolate families. For example, one mother participating in a focus group said, "I'm listening to people talk about their kids being included in a class picnic and I'm just happy if a day goes by that the school doesn't call me to come in because he's hiding under a chair in the classroom or throwing one at the teacher."

SOCIAL ISOLATION

Families protested the exclusion of their children from the social life that is so important in middle school. One mother said, "My daughter has never had a play date or been invited to a party. Maybe she would have, if she didn't spend her life in special education classes. That's why I want her in classes with regular kids."

In this focus group, several parents were moved to tears of sympathy and understanding when a mother said, "I have twins in the eighth grade. They are identical except that Nick is blessed with a great brain and a wonderful personality. He is also very good at sports. This year he is president of his class.

"His identical twin, Justin, is autistic. He has funny little tics and is socially awkward. My heart breaks seeing them together. I often grieve for what Justin might have been. When someone calls to invite Nick to a party, I say. 'I assume you want Justin, too.' They don't, but I shame them into it."

THE IMPORTANCE OF THE IEP IN INSTRUCTION

The fourth faulty assumption was that all the teachers actually read and followed the IEPs of the students with disabilities who were in their classes. Since the IEP contains instructional strategies and suggestions for dealing with student behavior in the classroom, failure to read it seems to be a loss all the way around. It was a shock to the researchers to find that not all the teachers agreed on the importance of the IEP nor the benefit of including students with disabilities in their general education classrooms.

One teacher said he purposely didn't read IEPs. "If I get too big a picture, sometimes I either feel sorry for them or I treat them differently. I don't want to get so emotionally involved in some of their lives that I'm not an effective educator."

Even in these enlightened schools, which were chosen because they included students with disabilities and their families so completely, at least one teacher did not believe in inclusion. He was adamant about it.

"So, I'm supposed to change up my curriculum and teach for different levels. These kids are put in a regular classroom so they feel like they're a part of the school as a whole. It's supposed to be less hurtful for their feelings, but when I'm giving one kid one lab and another kid another lab there's an obvious difference between the two. How does that feel? I think inclusion is not right for all kids."

A family member who confronted classroom teachers with attitudes like this ran the risk of making things worse instead of better. The whole focus group nodded in agreement when a parent said, "You make a big stink and you ruffle all the feathers and then you don't get the support you need because you're just the troublemaker."

Lorna's son, Seth, had recently been diagnosed with schizophrenia. Lorna, a single parent, reported that she also had schizophrenia and many of her extended family suffered from the same disease. Lorna was a frequent visitor to the school. She often sat in on Seth's classes, ready to help calm him down or lure him out from under his desk, the place where he took refuge when things in the classroom got to be too much for him.

Lorna was a woman with a mission. It was her decision to give Seth the opportunity to take two classes in mainstream classrooms, the first time he had ever experienced learning outside a sheltered setting. When she discovered that some of his teachers hadn't read Seth's IEP, she scheduled interviews with them to explain Seth, not just his disabilities but his intelligence, which tested near the genius range.

She brought homemade cookies to the interviews and gave the teachers what she called the *Reader's Digest* version of Seth's history. "When I don't get anywhere, I have to decide whether to push the issue. I have to ask myself, 'Is this the hill I want to die on?'"

DIFFICULT TRANSITIONS

During the three years of the research, the family focus groups became support groups, as family members bonded with one another over important issues in their children's lives. The first year, when their children were in seventh grade, the families talked about academic placement and achievement. The second year, concerns about the social acceptance of their children dominated the discussion. By the third year, the emphasis changed to discussions of the families' anxieties about transitioning their children to high school.

The move from middle school to high school is challenging for most students and their families, but for the families of students with disabilities those challenges are magnified. Will my child have friends? Will the teachers in a large high school understand the nature of my child's disability? How will my child feel when other students begin to drive and date and he or she cannot?

Little wonder then that families dreaded the transition process, perhaps even more than their children did. To help allay their fears, the researchers invited a counselor from the local high school to be a guest at one family focus group meeting. It soon became evident that she, a twenty-five-year veteran, was not prepared for what she heard.

An early topic was learning how to open students' lockers at the high school. The counselor laughed at first, saying, "Lots of kids have trouble with their lockers at the beginning of school." "But," one mother interrupted, "how many students have you had like my son, who, if he could not open his locker, would stand and bang his head against it until someone stopped him or he knocked himself out?"

The counselor started the evening confident that she could quell concerns about students getting lost in the large, labyrinthine high school. She began assuredly. "That happens all the time too. We give them maps and encourage them to ask any teacher for help. It's not a big deal."

"Not true," said a father in the group. "We have a daughter who would never ask for help. If she gets lost, she will just leave by the nearest exit and try to find her way home. It may take the police to get her back to us."

That counselor left with a new perspective on her role in the transition process. Long after the meeting ended, she and several members of the focus group stood outside the school chatting animatedly. She gave them all her cell phone number and offered private high-school tours for them and their children.

A PLACE FOR DAMON

Most families of students with disabilities see their children's strengths and potential and want them to be in general education classes. Not only do they think that their children can handle the instructional challenges, perhaps with help from an in-class aide, they also want their child to be socially accepted by students who do not have special needs.

As the students reach middle-school age, they too may want a say in the composition of their IEPs. Damon was an eighth-grader with a special education diagnosis of Attention Deficit Hyperactivity Disorder (ADHD).

Damon's family had just moved into the school district and his mother carried "battle scars" from her experiences with special education staff in her previous school district. The thing that outraged her most was that they wanted to put Damon on medication and she was convinced, based on her reading about the issue, that "white teachers just want little black boys on meds so they don't cause trouble."

Damon and his mother were both convinced that Damon could handle general education classes in every subject and Damon's case manager at his new school agreed to let him try. "That was my first surprise," Damon's mother said. "I talked, she listened. Usually, it's the other way around."

When Damon found he could not keep up with the work in social studies and science, he began hiding his homework from his mother because he didn't want her to know he was failing. Then he started getting into mischief in class and the assistant principal called Damon's mother. "I was ready for a fight," she said, but instead he suggested that Damon check in with him every morning, show him his completed homework assignments, and make a "handshake" promise not to get into trouble that day.

Damon's mother termed the assistant principal her "good angel" because his influence on Damon's behavior was so positive. At the same time, the case manager suggested that Damon make a choice between social studies and science. He could continue in one class as a general education student and would join a special education class for the other. Together, the case manager and his mother met with Damon and discussed what he wanted to do.

Until then, Damon had resisted special education classes. "I'm not a retard," was his tearful or belligerent response. But, given a chance to sit down with adults and face his challenges, Damon agreed to take science in a special education class and social studies in a general education class. "I love social studies," he said, and he did well in that class, even when the material was complex and challenging.

THE RESEARCH FINDINGS

The major outcome of the study was a better understanding of the factors that facilitated successful partnerships between schools and the families of students with disabilities. Each represents a dimension of an intentional decision on the part of the school leadership to create an inclusive community for the families and their children.

Melding of Visions. The core issue affecting the school/family relationship was neither a legal matter nor one of instruction, but rather one of conflicting visions. A school is likely to see students in terms of academic deficits and focus on remedies. The families see their children in terms of their gifts and abilities. The students likely just want to be seen as normal kids. The primary reason these schools were so successful is that they held everyone's vision to be valid, negotiated to find common ground, and eventually established a workable consensus.

Proactive, Authentic Communication. The school staff listened responsively to the opinions of students and their families. All parties to a conversation were committed to speaking frankly and hearing without prejudice. Staff phoned families with an "I am concerned" statement, not a "problem" statement.

Communication occurred immediately when there was an issue. Email was used for routine messages but not for problem solving. There was no one time, one place, or one person linking families or students to the school. Families were empowered to seek out a teacher, counselor, or administrator at any time.

Academic Challenge and Support. Students with disabilities were expected to perform at the highest levels they could achieve through the use of appropriate supports. The constant balancing and rebalancing of challenge and support was the throughline of planning instruction. Teachers and administrators sought continuously to find the ideal intersection of challenge and support for each individual student.

Inclusion. All students with disabilities were part of the school community and included in the social life of the school, such as clubs, teams, class trips, and school events. Staff kept an eye out for students who appeared socially isolated, talked to their families about it, and took steps to include them.

Aspirations. Students were encouraged to work toward their highest dream of the future. The school could not guarantee they would achieve all their ideals, but continuously provided assurance that they had the right to aspire.

Respect for Diversity. Respect for diversity was not equivalent to pretending that everyone is the same. People with different racial and linguistic backgrounds have different experiences, as do families whose children have severe disabilities. These schools celebrated the entire continuum of diversity.

Those who denigrate schools, teachers, and the public education enterprise often say that education is not rocket science. It's not. Actually, it is more challenging. The process for creating a rocket is an exact science and, if you follow it, the result will be a rocket. The process of educating children is an inexact science, subject to complex factors and countervailing forces. The result is never guaranteed. The schools in this study were committed to achieving the best possible results by integrating students with disabilities and their families into the process.

IN YOUR TOOLBOX

A copy of the evaluation tools that support this chapter, *IEP Meeting Participant Survey*, and *Survey of Teacher Attitudes toward Students with Disabilities*, appear in the appendix. They are also available for free per request to nbrighamassoc@yahoo.com.

Section Two

TEACHERS AND INSTRUCTION

Chapter 5

The Best Teachers

It began as a large-scale research study to examine the effects of certain instructional practices on student achievement and ended in a conundrum. The study was conducted with a national sample of seventy-one high-poverty elementary schools and focused on grades 3 through 5. These schools were early adopters of instructional practices that stemmed from the school reform movement, which hit its stride in the 1990s.

The instructional practices of interest in this study included project-based learning, active learning, and the design of more challenging tasks for students to build their higher-order thinking skills. The list of practices was drawn from an extensive literature search and had been validated in previous studies.

The hypothesis driving the research was that use of these practices would improve student achievement during the three years of data collection. The major data source for the study was an annual survey of all the K–5 teachers in the selected schools.

At the beginning of the study, the team conducting the research reviewed previous standardized test results for each school in the sample, classroom by classroom. In the process, they discovered nine elementary schools in which the students consistently and conspicuously outperformed their demographic peers. A closer look revealed that the high achievement scores were not schoolwide, but rather centered in twenty-one particular classrooms.

In these classrooms, students excelled in reading and math every year. No matter where the students scored on the achievement scale when they entered the classrooms, by the time they moved to the next grade, they exceeded academic expectations in reading, math, or both. The question, of course, was, how did the teachers get these positive results?

To find out, the funder of the study commissioned a set of individual case studies including classroom observations and interviews with the twenty-one teachers who, based on their students' test scores, were called "highly effective teachers." The survey addressed questions of how many teachers used specific practices and how often they did so, while the case studies contextualized the practices in action in individual classrooms.

The expectation was that the case studies would agree with the survey findings, but instead they contradicted them. The conundrum was that highly effective teachers had not adopted innovative instructional approaches but instead relied on practices seen as old fashioned and outdated by education reformers.

Practice and drill in the upper elementary grades was dubbed "drill and kill," but the highly effective fourth- and fifth-grade teachers actually did a lot of drill and the students seemed to thrive on it. Included in the "drill and kill" category were memorization and rote responses.

The highly effective teachers insisted on students memorizing the multiplication tables by rote. As one teacher said, "Students need to know their multiplication facts as quick as a snap because these facts are the basic tools for problem solving and mathematical literacy." Observers also saw frequent use of rote response to questions, including some choral responses. The students enjoyed shouting out their answers like fans responding to cheerleaders at a football game.

The highly effective teachers also spent a fair amount of time lecturing, which was, at the time, pejoratively called "stand and deliver." The lectures were not stand-alone lessons. Rather, they were part of a cycle that included the teachers modeling how to use the information and then assigning students guided practice. At this point in the cycle, students demonstrated in oral response or writing that they had grasped the information.

From the reform point of view, quizzes developed by teachers resulted in "testing students to death." Conversely, the highly effective teachers believed in frequent, even daily tests, to determine exactly what information students understood and what they did not. The frequent use of teacher-made tests was in fact one of the practices most often observed in the third-, fourth-, and fifth-grade classrooms of the highly effective teachers.

The observers of the highly effective teachers noted that the environment of the classroom and the leadership style of the teachers heightened and enhanced the use of specific instructional strategies. These two factors, environment and style, appeared to form the foundation for effective instruction. The observers reported that

- The highly effective teachers created an atmosphere that was safe, structured, and predictable;

- Students were protected from ridicule and free to take risks in offering their ideas or answers;
- Classroom management was a nonissue because students knew what behavior was expected of them and what was not allowed.

The purpose of conducting the case studies was not just to confirm or challenge the findings of the survey. There was also the hope that by learning what made the teachers so successful, the study results could help select and prepare teacher candidates and design more effective professional development for teachers already in the field.

MR. REDDING, FOURTH GRADE

Mr. Redding, whose fourth-grade students had excelled in both reading and math achievement, taught at a high poverty neighborhood school for many years. Although the school was small, it was a challenge to find his classroom. A long corridor held all the classes from grades 1 through 5, except for Mr. Redding's room.

The only other option for exploration was a shorter corridor to the left of the main office, which contained the nurse's office, the assistant principal's office, and a storage room. Then the hallway took an unexpected right turn, and there was Mr. Redding's classroom. He could not have isolated his class more completely without leaving the school entirely.

The school had experienced extensive principal turnover, turmoil among teaching staff, and crippling budget cuts, which resulted, according to one teacher, in "cutthroat politics" among the teachers in the long hallway. Mr. Redding decided it was bad for him and his students to be exposed to this negativity and simply picked up and moved to the classroom of his choice. After twenty-four years of teaching in the school and his stellar history of success, Mr. Redding was beyond censure.

The observer noted his reaction to a phone ringing in his classroom while he was demonstrating a new concept on the board. He glanced toward the phone but didn't answer it. A few minutes later, a disembodied voice on the loudspeaker said, "Mr. Redding, please call the office." He turned and said firmly to the loudspeaker: "Not now, I'm busy teaching."

The observer's seat in Mr. Redding's classroom was an uncomfortable straight chair next to his desk. He never sat at his desk, but when he circled back to pick up materials, he would occasionally stop and explain elements of his teaching style.

"Much of my teaching is about following directions, keeping a tidy desk, filing away your work, and respecting time and materials. Many of these students come from homes with little or no structure. Two of them are living with their families in their cars right now. It's important that they learn long division. It's more important that they learn the skills they need to succeed in life."

No detail was too small for Mr. Redding's attention. He had his students write their math examples on graph paper, leaving four squares between rows and columns, which made the paper easier for him and the student to read and, he believed, decreased the number of careless mistakes.

He did not use anthologies of short stories for reading practice, but rather filled his bookcase with slim paperback versions of single stories. He said he did that so that each time a student finished a story, the student had a feeling of accomplishment and motivation to move on to the next story.

He insisted that the students use sharp pencils. In one class, he said to a student, "A pencil that isn't sharp is not a workable tool." The student immediately got up, went to a tin can sitting on Mr. Redding's desk and got a workable tool, one of many sharp pencils Mr. Redding kept in readiness.

Project-based learning was a pillar of the new instructional practices, but Mr. Redding didn't use it with his students. "In this class, less than one-third of the students are reading on grade level or have basic computational skills. So, I ask myself, should I be doing something like projects that take a lot of time and teach a few things or should I stick to the basic concepts they must have? And, usually I come down on the side of teaching the basics."

Mr. Redding's students took a math warm-up test every morning. He explained, "I used to start teaching right off in the morning. Then I noticed that no one was paying attention. Now the students know they will get a warm-up test. It's a chance for the student to say, 'Oh, I remember. I'm in school. Good morning, brain. We're going to work now.'"

The interview with Mr. Redding at the conclusion of the three-day observation was terse and uninformative. He took control of the interview as firmly as he ruled his classroom. He asked for a copy of the questions in advance and brought the printed questions with him. The interview was scheduled to take forty-five minutes, but he bargained it down to thirty and it was over in twenty. He kept track of the progress of the interview, moving his thumb down the page from one question to another.

Experienced interviewers like an interview to achieve the easy flow of a natural conversation. An unexpected response may lead to new insights and so the interviewer may follow a new path and include questions that are not on the printed list. The questions, after all, are composed before knowing exactly what issues may arise on the site visit. The most informative interviews include more than rote answers to rote questions.

Mr. Redding obviously did not agree. One question was whether the teacher's life had included a mentor, someone whose influence or guidance contributed to his philosophy of teaching. He said, "No." That was it. To an interviewer, a monosyllabic answer is a challenge that demands a follow up. "Perhaps, some seminal event turned you toward teaching? Was there something like that?"

Since the question was not on the paper in front of him, he responded with the same quelling look that brought instant silence to his classroom. It was just as effective in ending any effort to stray from the questions on the list and the interview continued with the printed questions and brief answers.

UNSATISFACTORY CONCLUSIONS

Despite reams of notes and interview responses, the researchers came back from their first round of visits with more unanswered questions than conclusions. The postobservation interviews with other teachers were more generous, more genial, and more informative than the one with Mr. Redding, but it was still impossible to cull from the data what combination of circumstance and characteristics set these teachers apart from their peers.

How did the highly effective teachers create an environment of success? How did they establish high expectations, and how did they motivate every student to learn when many had experienced failure since they started first grade? What were the secrets of their classroom-management techniques?

The first round of visits had taken place in May when the teachers' expectations and the classroom culture were well embedded. Perhaps by observing the first few days of school in September, the magic would be made visible. Additional funding allowed a second round of visits to fifteen of the twenty-one teachers to determine how they established their expectations at the beginning of the year.

THE SECOND ROUND OF VISITS

In early September, back in Mr. Redding's classroom, a new set of fourth-graders started their year. Each student was ushered into the room individually and Mr. Redding made sure that each of them was seated at a desk that fit their height. He put some students in three different seats before he was satisfied that they were completely comfortable and could see the front blackboard.

All eyes were on Mr. Redding as he introduced himself. He was a big man, well over six feet tall, with a deep, resonant voice. He started by saying, "I run a really strict classroom. I don't have many rules, but the rules I have are the same for everyone. We are here to learn. Your success matters to me."

Over the heads of the students, he remarked to the observer. "It's my business to be engaged in teaching. It's their business to be engaged in learning. We get that straight at the beginning of the year and we don't have to revisit it."

Then he told the students, "Not everybody learns the same way, so I'll do things differently. I will try three or four ways to teach something. My job is to help you understand, and your job is to listen, pay attention, and learn. I'll stay with you as long as you need, even after school. Don't give up on yourself, because I will never give up on you.'"

He concluded by making a promise that carried a tinge of threat. "If I need to see your parents, I'll call them; go to your house, whatever it takes. I really like talking to parents to tell them that you are taking care of business and that you're doing well. If I need to talk to them about how to help you focus on your job of learning, then I will."

As he talked, students began to straighten up in their chairs, their body language demonstrating interest and attention. "In this classroom you are not allowed to say, 'I can't do it.' You can say; that this is a new task, that it is hard, that you don't yet know how to do something, or that you are afraid to try something for the first time, but you cannot say, 'I can't do this.'"

MR. BRUNO, FIFTH GRADE

The second visit that September was to Mr. Bruno's classroom. There was no first observation report since the original observer was not available. This was another high poverty neighborhood school where the only students scoring above expectations in both reading and math on national tests were the fifth-graders taught by Mr. Bruno. Like Mr. Redding, Mr. Bruno had taught in the same school for more than twenty years and he had turned down multiple opportunities to teach in schools with greater resources.

Mr. Bruno's classroom was in a sunlit corner of the school. He was a slight, soft-spoken man devoted to bringing out the best in each student and giving them a sense of safety. For students, safety means not just physically protected from violence, but emotionally secure. Mr. Bruno attempted to make every student in his class feel safe from ridicule and safe to make a mistake. He was not only a master teacher; he was also a master builder of emotional security and self-esteem.

At one point during the observation, he called on a student to answer a question. The student did not even have the book open to the right page. Patiently, Mr. Bruno directed him to the question. It took a minute because the student was flustered, but eventually he was able to answer the question adequately.

In his interview, Mr. Bruno said that the boy's mother was in drug rehab and the student worried about her. "It's hard for him to focus on his work right now," he said, "but what would I be teaching him if I just called on another student? He could go back to his daydreaming and he wouldn't have the boost to his self-esteem that he got from answering correctly and he wouldn't have learned anything."

On the morning of the first day of school, Mr. Bruno was busy putting the finishing touches to a poster on his classroom door. He explained, "I read last night that your door should say your name, some kind of welcome, and the children's names, so I put all of this on here."

The colorful poster showed his name, each of the students' names, and WELCOME spelled out in big letters. The students reacted just as he hoped, stopping at the door, finding their names and their friends' names and entering the classroom already relaxed and positive. It was impressive that after so many years of teaching Mr. Bruno was still finding innovative ways to welcome his new students.

Like Mr. Redding, he made it clear that no matter what the students' home circumstances, he had high expectations of them and of himself. "I am aware that many of my fifth-grade students have difficult home lives. I feel very sympathetic with the things they face, but it's still important that they come to school to learn. That's what school is for and I am their teacher. My job is to show them that they can learn, not to offer them an alternative setting."

As soon as the class assembled, Mr. Bruno began, "My name is Terry Bruno. I've been teaching for twenty-five years. I consider myself a good teacher. When I say that, I mean that I try to help every student to be successful. My reward is to see you grow both academically and socially."

A few classroom rules were posted on the board and he went through them one by one to explain their importance. "Classroom rules are very important and the best one is the golden rule. All other rules hinge on that."

When he asked the students if they knew the golden rule, all but one student looked blank. The one volunteer said that the golden rule is "not falling asleep in class." Mr. Bruno acknowledged solemnly that not falling asleep was a very good rule, but not the golden rule. He then explained that the golden rule is "treating people as you want them to treat you."

He encouraged his students to elaborate on the implications of the rule, letting the discussion go on for a full seven minutes. Whatever else the students remembered from their first day of fifth grade, they all probably went home knowing and perhaps understanding the golden rule.

Mr. Bruno had few rules, but he consistently reinforced them. He used after-school detention as a disciplinary tool. One day, during the observation, a student who had been assigned to detention skipped out after school and went home. When Mr. Bruno noticed, he simply walked to the student's house, knocked on the door and when the student opened it, he said, "You're walking back to school with me. You owe me a detention."

Mr. Bruno used his morning tests, sometimes math and sometimes vocabulary, as instructional tools and carefully reviewed the answers with the students. When a student answered incorrectly, he called on the next student. But then he always went back to the first student and asked him to repeat the correct answer. Mr. Bruno explained. "I don't want the last thing they hear themselves say to be inaccurate."

MR. WARDEN, THIRD GRADE

Mr. Warden's third graders excelled only in math achievement. His students' scores in reading were average. During each of the observations, Mr. Warden spent more time on math than was on his schedule and less time on reading and writing. It was obvious that math was his passion. It was not just the extra time but the enthusiasm Mr. Warden generated that probably motivated students to high achievement.

Like Mr. Redding and Mr. Bruno, Mr. Warden spent time the first day of school making his expectations clear to students. Before class, he said to the observer, "The reason that establishing expectations for behavior is so important is that most of these students want to learn and they can't if the structure is not there to facilitate learning. The key is structure, structure, structure. They have to know this is how a paper looks, this is where your name goes, this is how you will number and label the problems."

Mr. Warden's first-day discussion with students emphasized personal responsibility. He said, "Third grade is the time when you have to learn neatness, completeness, and a sense of personal responsibility. When you're in the third grade, it's time to take responsibility for yourself, not to wait to have everything done for you."

The students were wide eyed and attentive as Mr. Warden continued, "One of the most important things I have learned as a teacher is not to accept excuses. Your homework is your responsibility. A note from your parents will not excuse you. If you don't bring your homework back, you will miss the first recess. That's it. No excuses!" Later, he said he may have sounded harsh, but that he believed that "Homework is for practice, but it is mainly to teach responsibility."

The students were eager to be chosen for one of the many helper roles in the classroom, another tactic to instill a sense of personal responsibility. The chores were structured and precise. There were nine altogether, ranging from turning the lights on and off to carrying the recycling bin to the cafeteria. By far the most popular task for which all the students raised their hands was bringing vegetables from the cafeteria to Posy, the guinea pig.

Previous classes must have been very generous with Posy since she was as round as a barrel and about as animated. Nonetheless, the students often stopped by her cage and said a few words to her. Posy undoubtedly heard a lot of secrets, but her only reaction was the occasional twitch of her nose.

Mr. Warden was persnickety about details. Each time the students left the room, he insisted on a well-spaced, straight line and if they didn't get it right the first time, they had to line up again and even a third or fourth time. A coveted daily chore was to be the leader of the line and make expansive hand gestures to direct other students to their places. Rather than resenting this approach, the students seemed to enjoy the process and to be proud of getting it right.

Mr. Warden administered a warm-up arithmetic test each morning, which gave him a daily data point for each student. He said, "The most important word in the phrase 'supportive learning environment' is learning and that's what I'm all about." A lover of data, he kept extensive statistics on each individual student and used test results to enrich his understanding of students' progress, strengths, and weaknesses.

A page in his grade book was allotted to each student, showing the acquisition of critical skills and individual progress. He shared the data with students and hoped they would develop an interest in statistics. Third grade may seem a little young for this, but good teachers can interest students in almost anything.

Mr. Warden also kept families informed about the academic progress of their children. Every two weeks, he sent home a mini report card based on a program that provided a complete grading system for every child in every subject showing points earned, missing assignments, and grades on assignments.

It is poignant that Mr. Warden seemed to think that everyone was as enamored of statistics as he was. Parents may well have encountered trouble deciphering the many elements of the report card; they might have preferred a "Johnny did well" or a set of A's and B's, but it would never have satisfied Mr. Warden.

MS. TOBIN, MIXED FOURTH AND FIFTH GRADE

Ms. Tobin was a veteran teacher in an urban school. The neighborhood around the school was one of the few economically depressed areas in an otherwise thriving city. For many years, Ms. Tobin's fourth-graders have surpassed expectations in standardized tests of both math and reading. The year she was observed, she was teaching a combined fourth and fifth grade, sharing her students with the teacher across the hall. Again, the original observer was not available for the second visit.

During the first week of school, Ms. Tobin phoned the family of each child in her class to ask how their children felt about the beginning of the school year. She also wrote a letter introducing herself and spelling out classroom expectations. As she noted, "It's really important to communicate with parents to develop a positive connection to school and to me. This sets the tone for communication later in the school year. Then, if there are problems, you have the parents' involvement and support."

The first day of school in Ms. Tobin's class was quite different from those of the male teachers. While the male teachers established communities with themselves at the center, Ms. Tobin created an inclusive community of students of which she was a member, albeit the member with the final word when it came to instruction and discipline.

Community meetings involving all students took place daily in Ms. Tobin's classroom. A red carpet at the front of the room was reserved for this use. On the first day of school, she immediately convened the students on the carpet. Before class, she told the observer that through her behavior and her language, she wanted students to learn that she valued honesty, the work ethic, and the ability to learn.

In the community meeting, Ms. Tobin invited the students to discuss agreements about behavior so that all of them would "feel comfortable and safe to share experiences." The students agreed unanimously that they shouldn't laugh at other students, shouldn't bully, should keep their hands to themselves, and should listen attentively to others.

Immediately after the meeting, the teacher organized a listening game that helped to demonstrate the agreements. Each group of three students had a speaker, a listener, and an observer. The speaker read aloud from a story provided by Ms. Tobin. The listener's task was to be attentive. Afterward, the student assigned as the observer described to the class the positive things he or she observed as well as what behaviors hindered attentive listening, and what students might do to make it better.

Ms. Tobin listed their responses on a white board. They encompassed: not zoning out, making eye contact, giving some verbal indication that you're listening, and not fidgeting. She explained in her interview that this particular activity had multiple purposes: to build inclusion; that is, all children should be heard when they speak; to foster cooperation and participation; and to develop a cohesive spirit in the class.

On the second day of school, Ms. Tobin told the class that they would all have "classy jobs." The class president checked returned homework with parent's signatures, and the secretary gave out stickers for work well done. As she assigned jobs, Ms. Tobin continued to urge students to help one another.

Ms. Tobin belonged to the school of small gestures and invisible discipline. In her class, you had to watch closely to see discipline happen. For example, during the reading lesson, she caught the eye of an inattentive student and simply pointed to the list of attentive listening strategies on the easel. That's all it took and the student who was reading aloud was not distracted by time spent disciplining another student.

During reading time, Ms. Tobin had groups of students come to read with her in the back of the room. One boy in the group tilted his chair back on two legs. Without interrupting her reading, Ms. Tobin touched his knee and he brought the chair down at once.

Another boy, apparently forgetting a hard-and-fast rule, walked over to sharpen his pencil while other students were reading aloud. Ms. Tobin shook her head no more than a fraction of an inch at him, and he clapped himself on the forehead (what a dunce I am!) and returned to his seat.

Ms. Tobin was an astute and creative teacher. Her fifth-grade math class included three boys whose abilities far surpassed those of the other students. As the class engaged in oral responses to mental math puzzles, these boys were quicker than anyone else and became quite boisterous about their superiority.

Other students' shoulders were slumping and it seemed that the class was about to yield to the three boys and let them do all the problems. Ms. Tobin saw what was happening and suggested that the three boys go to the back of the room and compete against the rest of the class. The class against the boys; everyone loved the idea.

Huddled together over a counter in the back of the room, the three boys worked incredibly hard and cooperatively to solve problems. The rest of the class practically broke into a sweat trying to figure out the greatest number of answers. The competition was fierce and now involved every student. The boys group did indeed come up with more answers than the class, but Ms. Tobin played down the victory cheers and assured the whole group they had done well.

Ms. Tobin's passion was reading. "I want students each day to have an extended period of time to really engage with a book of their choice. I do all kinds of mini lessons on how to select books, how to be an active reader, making connections with the text, and using questioning techniques. They learn how to select a book that is just the right reading level for them."

Unlike the three male teachers, Ms. Tobin did not begin the day with a quiz. Instead, when students arrived each morning, they were expected to self-select a book, settle down comfortably with it somewhere in the room, and read without interruption for a period of thirty-five minutes. "The only noise in the room" Ms. Tobin said, "will be whispering that I will do with another reader as we read together or talk about how their book is going for them."

While the male teachers emphasized structure and routine as the foundation of good instruction, Ms. Tobin said that respect was the most important thing. "I know they will come to respect me. For many of them, respect for adults is not a part of their home lives. If they're going to learn it at all, they will learn it in school."

CONCLUSIONS FROM THE DATA

When the research team met yet again to analyze the total set of data from two rounds of visits, the first finding was that male teachers comprised a disproportionate number of the highly effective elementary school teachers observed in the case studies. Almost half the teachers in the sample were men, even though male teachers generally comprise less than 20 percent of the teaching force in elementary and middle schools.

There are many superb women teachers in elementary schools and, in fact, several of them were part of this study. Elementary-grade teaching remains a default profession for a woman and a nontraditional decision for a man. Thus, a man who chooses to teach in elementary school is making it his mission. One of the male teachers in the study addressed this phenomenon directly. "A lot of kids need a male role model, especially at this age. I think about that every day, and I know that that is why I am here."

Learning from men is unusual for children in poverty whose lives are likely to be surrounded by women. Single-parent homes are most often headed by mothers and grandmothers. For some students, a male teacher is the first father figure they have ever encountered except on television. These teachers filled a missing piece in their lives that the students might not even have recognized themselves.

The final set of case studies of the highly effective teachers showed the importance of clear roles and relationships. They defined and modeled these at the beginning of the year:

- No matter what their home circumstances, students came to school to learn;
- An explicit commitment that all the students in their classroom would succeed; and
- The investment must be total on both sides. Just as the teachers made a commitment to them, the students must make a commitment to themselves.

Beyond that, the data showed few clear patterns. Most of the highly effective teachers never had mentors or memorable experiences that led them into teaching or to teach the way they did. The effect of professional development on their style and method of teaching was minimal. In fact, the most frequent response was that they learned how to teach through trial and error.

At the time, the answer was frustrating. In retrospect, as the use of "best instructional practices" has become a universal expectation rather than an option; teachers have less freedom to match instructional strategies to student needs. Teachers, under scrutiny by administrators or enmeshed in new policies embraced by the school district, feel obliged to showcase the latest initiatives and the most recent set of best practices, whether or not they understand when to use them or how to use them effectively.

The results of the survey research were that use of the innovative practices did not result in any positive change in student achievement at any grade level in either reading or math. The expected correlation didn't occur. During the same three years, however, the highly effective teachers continued to post high achievement scores, even though they were using relatively traditional methods of instruction.

One explanation for the difference between the surveys and the case studies stems from a weakness of the survey research, which depended entirely on teachers' self-report of their use of the practices. Without more information, it was difficult to know if teachers implemented the practices completely and correctly.

In terms of implementing the new instructional practices, a lot depended on the quality of the professional development the teachers had received and extent to which they believed in changing practice. A challenge to professional development at that time was that the instructional approaches that emerged from the school reform movement were abstract and complicated.

They differed from the norm of strategies that characterized professional development in the past. The professional-development sessions did not satisfy the teachers who were seeking immediately usable information or what Michael Huberman memorably called "recipes for busy kitchens."[1]

A more recent evaluation of professional development shows that teachers are still looking for the practical advice they can use in their classrooms tomorrow. A teacher in that study said, "It is not just theory I want to learn, it is more practical classroom information." Another said, "The workshop activities are all well and good on paper, but in our situation, with students reading/writing well below grade level, with little to no motivation, there is very little use for advanced activities like these."

The observations of the best teachers reveal that it is not a matter of innovative versus traditional teaching methods, but of innovative *and* traditional teaching methods, used to fit the needs of the students. Trial and error is a tool, not a failure, and when teachers learn through their own actions what works and what doesn't, they and their students will benefit.

NOTE

1. Michael Huberman, "Recipes for Busy Kitchens," *Knowledge: Creation, Diffusion, Utilization* 4 (1983): 478–510.

Chapter 6

Professional Development

Large Investment, Limited Results

Professional development in education covers a wide array of activities, from individual facilitators doing after-school workshops at one end of the continuum, to multidistrict, multistate symposia offered by people famous in their field at the other end. It is intended to provide knowledge and skills for teachers already working in the field and to be a catalyst for change. Professional development is also charged with introducing and facilitating new teaching practices at the classroom level. The ultimate goal is to increase student learning and engagement.

To make professional development effective, it is critical to be cognizant of three issues: understanding teachers' priorities; helping teachers to learn from and with each other; and understanding the complex cultures of schools. These issues apply to every type or model of professional development.

MEETING TEACHERS WHERE THEY ARE

Workshops. A popular model is the workshop, in which a professional trainer or facilitator presents a program or approach that is being introduced, implemented, or reinforced in some set of schools. For teachers, the most important factors of workshop training are the credentials of the trainer, and what can they do with the information they receive.

It is important for the facilitator to have an in-depth understanding of the audience. A fairly typical example of the workshop model is the Complete Literacy Program (CLP) that was implemented in several low-performing high schools in an urban school district.

Credentials. The trainer representing CLP was an expert in literacy, but the first question asked at each school was some variation of, "Do you have classroom experience?" No matter what expertise or reputation a professional development specialist brings to the work, teachers want to know that the facilitator has been in the trenches and taught students like theirs.

Whether it's fair or not, the classroom credential establishes the level of trust teachers bring to the training. Of the CLP facilitator, a teacher said, "She knows what it's like in the classroom. She's an educated woman, but she's also street savvy."

Method. In addition to her twenty-five years in the classroom, the teachers appreciated the CLP's facilitator's approach to communicating with them. One teacher described previous professional development in the school. "Facilitators who come here from other programs tell us to be very creative with the kids and then don't give us a chance to do anything. They're talking and talking and talking. They show you a video, they show you something. You can hardly see it, but you say 'Uh-huh, uh-huh.' Then you go home.

"But when you leave the CLP workshops, you feel happy. You really feel good when you leave. You go in with one strategy and you leave with two more. The facilitator told one of the teachers she would walk in to her classroom and teach her class. We totally believed she would do it too."

Another said, "She teaches by example. When I realized how important it is to me that the facilitator gets us up and moving in our after-school workshops, it occurred to me that I need to do the same thing with my kids. It's just as important for keeping them engaged."

Although the facilitator only met with each group of teachers once a month, she maintained accountability. "I think she keeps records on what the previous meetings were about and she follows up on that. She'll ask us if we applied what we learned and if not, why not.

"She follows through with the various things we've done, so we all took turns saying, 'I did this' and tell her that it worked or it didn't. If it didn't, she often offers to come to your classroom to observe where the activity went wrong."

Use of the Information. The CLP facilitator's philosophy was: "If teachers attend a professional development workshop on Tuesday after school, I want them to leave with something they can use in the classroom Wednesday morning." Teachers appreciated this approach. "When I leave the sessions I think more outside the box. It is not just theory it is more practical classroom information."

Another teacher said that an activity she learned on Tuesday helped her that same week to teach the play *Romeo and Juliet* more effectively. She said it marked the first time her low-achieving students really grasped the play.

School administrators were especially pleased with the response of veteran teachers to the work of the CLP facilitator because it "shakes up" their well-entrenched classroom practice and because these teachers are often powerful opinion shapers in the school. Another administrator said that CLP reminds teachers that "everybody is a literacy teacher and gives them tools to back up that claim."

Teacher Attitudes. Attendance at professional-development activities may be required of all teachers in the district or focused on teachers in certain schools. Teachers may be grouped by level; elementary, middle, and high school, or by subject. They may be a reluctant or a willing audience to what is being taught to them.

For example, Thayer Middle School became involved in a federally funded initiative to include students with disabilities in general education classes. These classes would be cotaught with special education teachers. The math teachers were generally quiet during the initial professional-development sessions, which included both the math teachers and the special education teachers.

In interviews with the evaluator, however, the math teachers gave voice to the feelings they had not wanted to express publicly. "The special education students have trouble with the curriculum because they are lacking the basic reasoning skills to go there in their heads. I don't mean to cut them down, but cognitive ability is what it is and you can take them to a point, but after that you're just getting frustrated and they are not going to get past that point."

In this instance, professional development continued over a three-year period and included biweekly study groups comprised of math and special education teachers led by skilled facilitators. As time went on, the teachers realized that many of their disagreements stemmed from the math teachers' devotion to content, and the special education teachers' focus on making the curriculum accessible to a range of students. Eventually, the two sets of teachers learned to compromise and to accept that both content and access were integral to teaching their students effectively.

At one meeting during the second year of the project, a special education teacher asked, "I wonder, do our students with disabilities really need to understand the derivation and significance of *pi* or do they just need to know how to use it?"

There was a hush while the math teachers digested this question because understanding the significance of *pi* is a vital element of the math curriculum. Finally, one math teacher said, "No, I guess they don't," a truly immense change in attitude since the beginning of the project.

In terms of teacher attitudes, required attendance at professional-development events means that at least some teachers are going to arrive at the session unmotivated. Unless the presenter proves very engaging or the information seems important to them, the teachers simply zone out.

The facilitator must beware of teachers learning new activities but not tying them to the important concepts they illustrate. Picture a professional development session, where some fifteen elementary school teachers were running around the room, each trying to keep a ping pong ball in the air by blowing through a straw.

When everyone ran out of breath, the instructor reminded them that the point of the activity was to illustrate Bernoulli's principle. However, none of the teachers could put into words what the principle was or how the activity demonstrated it. Nevertheless, they loved the activity. One said, "When my principal sees me doing that, I'll probably get a gold star. Our school is based on show, don't tell."

The advent of laptop computers has made it possible for attendees to look engaged as they appear to take notes on what the presenter is saying, while in fact they are reading and answering emails or even playing solitaire. The presenter at the front of the room doesn't know what's going on of course, but anyone seated at the back of the room can assess audience interest by counting off-task laptop users.

Some of the planners of professional-development activities at the district level may appreciate the difficulty of engaging teachers in lively and informative sessions. However, they are frustrated by administrators above them in the district hierarchy who focus on cramming as much information as possible into the least amount of time.

One such planner, working with a group of administrators to plan professional development around a new state mandate said, "I found the process really clouded, disjointed, with many false starts. There were long meetings at the end of the day or during the summer."

"The focus kept changing because people joined or dropped out." The planner added, "It's purgatory being forced to sit at a table where people who don't understand the issues make assumptions about what we need."

Another planner said that she and someone from the high school had met to create a professional development plan and come to consensus about it. She said, "Such nice ideas if we had all the authority, time, and money in the world. It makes you want to stick needles in your eyes."

TEACHERS LEARNING FROM AND WITH EACH OTHER

A frequently used form of professional development is teachers meeting together on a regular basis to discuss student progress, to investigate new approaches to instruction, or to review data. Often, these groups are formed as a key component of implementing change in a school or schools districtwide.

The power of collaborative teacher groups is the synergistic effect of teachers being able to discuss and address issues on which they may have differing ideas or to tackle schoolwide instructional or behavioral issues.

Learning how to work together means developing collaboration skills and trust, even around difficult issues. However, these groups need accountability and support in order to keep on track and focused on instruction.

Collaborative Planning. Bolton Middle School teachers wanted to do more interdisciplinary units but found them difficult to plan. An interdisciplinary unit is a single topic that is covered simultaneously in math, science, social studies, and language arts. They agreed that the topic of weather is a good and easy subject to tackle. They dedicated themselves to more integration because "integration will help kids to retain information."

A major digression in this group meeting was about outings or field trips. One teacher remarked that "Ms. Green, the principal, loves field trips," and they talked about how she disliked having a performance incentive, for example, not letting students go on a trip because of their behavior or the level of their work. The teachers were not completely on board with this but decided to try it out. They reached a consensus not to argue with the principal on the issue.

Teachers in a study group in another school, which was involved in the same school-reform initiative, met as often and worked as hard as the teachers at the Bolton School. However, these teachers apparently took on an issue that was so large and pervasive in their school that they could not really get their arms around it. The subject was developing a schoolwide discipline policy.

When they tackled the issue during the first year, the goal was to tackle the school discipline code and revamp it. The following year, the object of their efforts was to "go back to the drawing board on classroom management" and find ways for teachers to handle more discipline on their own. Again, the second year, the issue consumed all the group's time and energy.

On the one hand, the importance of a consistent discipline policy in the school could not be ignored. On the other hand, the principal had hoped the group would get to academic issues during the second year and they never did. He, however, did not step in to refocus the group nor to suggest they bite off a smaller piece of policy.

A Risk-Free Zone. The principal of Sheridan School said that the major strength of the teacher-collaboration model was that it allowed "Asking the hard questions and discussing them without blame." She believed that using collaboration to implement practices that directly improve instruction is key to creating a successful school. "The teachers have to have those conversations together before they can own the work."

The principal of Andrews Middle School said, "I think it's like the grit, the sand that makes the pearl. If we don't have that back and forth rubbing up against each other and not agreeing, then we won't have a polished piece."

"I don't want to dance around. I want to get engaged in a discussion about why you are making the choices you're making and help me to see it from your point of view. I trust you, I admire you, I respect you and, you can win me to your side. I want to have that kind of dialogue in our study groups."

These administrators understood and supported the work of the teacher study groups in their schools. They held them accountable for having the hard conversations, tackling the big issues, and resolving conflict openly.

Trust. After two years of meeting with her colleagues in a weekly teacher study group, the seventh-grade social studies teacher at Morgan Middle School confided that she felt her instruction was hampered by her habit of "going off on tangents," and her ineffective time management. She asked her husband to videotape a class and then she showed the video to the members of her teacher study group for their advice and feedback.

One of the other group members called this "an awesome act of trust." Each member of the group was flattered to be consulted on such an important and personal issue and contributed constructive comments. The principal said, "Maybe she did it to address her own needs, but this one act has made the whole school a more collaborative place."

Some schools, however, whether through lack of training or failure to develop trust, let the collaborative groups lapse over time from discussing important issues into talking about trivial subjects.

For example, teacher study groups still meet regularly at Carson School. One teacher at Carson reported that her team met on Thursdays during the day, and they typically discussed student behavior, held parent conferences, and discussed referrals to special education. At a recent meeting, the topics included student recognition day and an upcoming field trip. They no longer discuss ways to improve instruction.

What changed? The previous principal had made the teacher study group accountable by asking for notes from each meeting. He had also dropped in on sessions occasionally to discuss some instructional issues. The new principal has no interest in the teacher study group and left the teachers to revert gradually to business as usual.

UNDERSTANDING THE COMPLEX
CULTURE OF SCHOOLS

Andrews University received a large federal grant to partner with eight local economically depressed middle and high schools. Andrews proposed recruiting and training experienced middle- and high-school math and science teachers to enhance their skills in Science, Technology, Engineering, and Math (STEM). The second and equally important purpose was to increase the leadership skills of the participants.

The school administrators in the partner school districts were enthusiastic about the purposes of the program, especially the idea of exposing teachers to the cutting edge of technology. One middle-school principal commented: "Twenty-five percent of the science questions on the state standardized test involve technology." Another said, "We live in a world where the technology gap is greater than the literacy gap."

Unlike many professional development initiatives, the STEM program did not require teachers to report back to other teachers at their schools or their principals about what they were learning. Some did; some didn't. The program staff also did not communicate with the schools very effectively. They largely used email, which administrators tended to overlook.

As part of an evaluation of the STEM program, visits were made to the administrators of the participating schools. A topic of interest during the visits was to understand what the administrators in the participating schools knew about the program, including the curriculum and activities that the teachers were experiencing.

Few school administrators were able to articulate the purpose of the STEM program or what was expected of the teachers as a result of their training. Several principals' comments illustrate the tenuous nature of their understanding.

• How long is the program? What will they come out with?
• I believe the program is associated with the zoo.
• It's tough to ferret it out.
• I don't know what they are getting from the program.

One principal gave a thoughtful response that focused on the loss of opportunity that occurred because the school administrators did not know what their teachers were doing in the program. "I could better tap into what they have learned if I had any idea what they are getting from the program. If I knew what the focus was, I could push them where they want to go. If I knew what they were getting, I could exploit their capacity. We would like to utilize their skills."

A dilemma for the schools and teachers was that taking part in the conferences and professional development opportunities offered by the program entailed being out of their classrooms more frequently than they and their school administrators believed was good for their students. The principal reported, "There is a strain on the school when the classroom teacher goes away. Right now, the students have had a sub for almost a week."

The concept of teacher leaders in the STEM program was broad, but not especially deep. The program defined as leadership skills everything from increasing the teachers' own fund of knowledge to creating a path to becoming administrators.

The leadership activities undertaken by the STEM teachers in their own schools remained close to the core of teaching and learning, such as developing curriculum, providing professional development for other teachers, and serving on schoolwide committees. The principals were very positive about these endeavors, even if they did not understand the possible contribution of the STEM program to leadership development. In the interviews, the principals made comments such as:

- The teacher participating in the STEM program is a Curriculum Leader in the school.
- He has been particularly active in selecting and adapting science curriculum.
- She wrote the new chemistry benchmark.
- The STEM teachers are particularly active in curriculum development.
- They are willing to help out with developing common assessments.
- She is very vocal in meetings about using data to plan curriculum.

UNIVERSITY/SCHOOL DISTRICT PARTNERSHIPS

A university and a school district enter into a partnership successfully when: (A) The university faculty sees school administrators as equals; (B) The university does not see itself as the sole repository of knowledge; (C) University faculty understand the exigencies of working in the K–12 education system; (D) All of the above.

The answer is D. The case of Kingston University is one that demonstrates a worst-case scenario of what happens when all these guidelines are ignored. The Kingston Leadership Program was funded by a major foundation and brought together the Kingston Faculty and leadership teams from a dozen states and their largest districts.

One component and a highlight of a much larger program was a three-day institute held on the Kingston campus in June. The program was innovative. Rather than an institute conducted by educators, the leaders and lecturers came from the university's business school. The participants were really excited about the institute, recognizing that a state department of education or a school district is a commercial as well as an instructional entity.

One superintendent said, "I am interested in the business aspects of education; in particular, how business and education can work together. I don't think that everything in business works in education because we're not producing widgets. There can be no one formula for success in education, however, I hoped to benefit from the expertise of the business faculty."

The retreat began on a beautiful June morning with flowers and trees blooming all around the campus. However, the sessions were all held in a windowless, over-air-conditioned amphitheater with the seats arranged in ascending rows. Participants sat like individual audience members and the team aspect was lost from the beginning.

The presenting business school faculty had decided to use case studies of various business ventures, which they then translated into issues facing administrators in education. The first session was called "Broadening the Constituent Base."

An assistant professor of business administration led a discussion about what happened when a product advertised as all-natural began to create E. coli-like symptoms in people who consumed it. Who are the company's constituencies? What strategies must the company use to reach each constituency? What messages need to be conveyed? How do you deal with a crisis?

The district teams went into breakout sessions to figure out how to deal with crises that arise in education concerning constituents, such as parents or the school board. They came up with some good questions:

* What do you do if a school is being taken over by the state?
* How do you deliver the message to families?
* What if it is in the best interests of the students?
* When there is a problem with the high-school graduation rate, how do you frame the discussion in positive terms?

The answers that district teams suggested were nowhere near as profound as the questions, perhaps because the presenter's case study provided no answers on how the company that was threatened by E. coli had dealt with their issue. The districts suggested as solutions: "Write a letter to families" and "Find a friendly reporter."

The theme of the next day's activities was "Development as Metaphor." All the presenters were in some way related to fundraising for the university and none of them explained the meaning of the phrase "development as metaphor."

The first of three presenters started out on a Socratic foot. He asked, "What is development?" and elicited the answers; fundraising, connections, relationships, and contributing. He then said that "development is not about raising money. It starts with the mission," which he described as building trust and demonstrating stewardship.

His mention of the word "mission" and the following speaker's urging to "think of the idea of creating an image of your schools" led the district teams to focus on their vision and mission statements during their forty-five-minute breakout sessions. The assignment was to "look at the message you are giving to constituents," which is a broader issue than the vision and mission statements, but none of the districts construed it that way.

Every day after lunch, one of the participating districts presented a report on the success of the program in their district. These papers were so completely couched in Education Speak that it was very difficult to figure out anything about success. For example, one report said:

> Implementing the principles of the program has brought many challenges, many changes, and many lessons. In order to continue the progress that has been made, our district must remain focused, consistently monitoring the projects as well as the process. Preparation is the key to a successful and efficient process. Keeping these lessons in mind, we will continue to improve district effectiveness and student achievement.

The overall theme of the third day was "Sustaining Constituents." The first presenter, a business school professor, presented a case study concerning an exploration team's trek through the Arctic and the many hardships they faced.

At the beginning of the case, there was a reference to a decision about whether to bring weapons in case they were attacked by polar bears. The polar bears played a minor role in a litany of hardships, but somehow the session ended up being mostly about polar bears.

This is where the retreat went off the rails and never really regained momentum. The mention of polar bears sent the participants into a metaphorical frenzy. When the presenter asked teams what they gleaned from the case, the questions and comments were these:

- "Who are your polar bears? You need to make connections with them."
- "Learn about your polar bears; assess them."
- "Outsmart them."
- "They are underground, watching."
- "Find common interests."

This was obviously not the point of the story and eventually the professor got the group back to the key questions and points he had put on the board and sent them into breakout groups with the following questions: "What are the actions that help you overcome obstacles? Who can help you? How will you engage potential helpers?" Many of the district teams came back to the session, still focused on polar bears. For example, they had written on their poster boards comments like this: "Identify the polar bears"; "Invite the polar bears to participate"; "Use all societal resources, including polar bears."

How did one paragraph in a long study of leadership and collaboration end up permeating the discussion, especially since the explorers didn't actually encounter any polar bears? It apparently also baffled the presenter, who left the building as soon as his session ended.

Not all the presentations during these three days missed the mark, but many did and the districts and the presenters were almost never on the same page. By day three, only about half the original district representatives attended and many of the attendees were using their laptops to check and reply to emails.

The waste of resources and time was staggering. Had the business school staff who planned the retreat done so in partnership with some of the district administrators, they might have put together a different retreat, one perhaps not so steeped in business metaphor. But this was one of those instances when the university assumed they were the leaders and reduced the participants to passive recipients of knowledge.

Any form or model of professional development can be successful. A skilled and lively facilitator can inspire teachers to learn and try out new instructional approaches. Teacher study groups that are supported and held accountable will learn with and from each other. If universities are willing to meet public school teachers and administrators on a platform of parity, these endeavors can enrich both partners' fund of knowledge.

IN YOUR TOOLBOX

A copy of the evaluation tools that support this chapter, *Teachers' Retrospective Judgment of the Usefulness of Professional Development* and *The Quality of Professional Development Activities* appear in the appendix. They are also available for free download per request to nbrighamassoc@yahoo.com.

Chapter 7

Angels of Special Education

You don't often run into angels in a research study, but the study of students with disabilities at Tyler High School revealed a special education staff who taught, nurtured, and enlivened their students' lives. Families felt blessed by the teachers' attitudes, which were rare in their experience. The parents believed that they had found the good angels of education.

Carol's mother, Lorraine, said she had been fighting the special education establishment since Carol started school. The syndrome that Carol suffered from is very rare and only a few thousand children in the world have been diagnosed with it. Lorraine keeps in touch with parents of other similarly disabled children through the Internet and has read extensively on the symptoms and treatment.

The symptoms include difficulty in processing information, which is the reason why Carol has a special education label, but Lorraine insists that Carol can handle mainstream education classes. She hates to see Carol in sequestered special education classes, but until Carol reached Tyler High School, Lorraine was not able to "get anyone to listen to me."

To make sure that Carol got additional academic support, her parents hired private tutors for her in math and reading. Lorraine said that she was prepared to take on the special educators at Tyler by using evidence from academic testing that the family had done privately. They also could bring to the table testimony from her tutors and, if necessary, Lorraine was willing to try "begging, pleading, and threatening."

But no fighting was necessary. Carol and Lorraine had walked into a school where students were offered many different models of special education support. This was a school in which the special education teachers appeared to spearhead the philosophical approach to instruction, which focused on the inclusion of all students in every area of academic and extracurricular activities.

The special education director made sure that all general education teachers had copies of the IEPs for students in their classes and had read them. Also, the special education department attempted to ensure the best environment for special education students through doing their class schedules by hand, rather than by computer, which is the default process.

The special education teachers sometimes handpicked the general education teachers to instruct some inclusion students based on their knowledge of the students' strengths and learning styles. Three special education options offered a continuum of support for students.

MAINSTREAM MONITORING

Many students with disabilities were placed in classrooms without direct support from special education teachers. To assist general education teachers in differentiating instruction to meet the needs of students at all levels, the special education department did professional development training on strategies and accommodations. The sessions took place once a month during planning periods for faculty members who were free at that time.

Special education teachers kept systematic track of the progress of students with disabilities who were enrolled in mainstream classes without special education support. Twice a semester, all the general education teachers submitted reports on every IEP student they had in class. They reported on the students' academic progress, conduct, and work effort.

Since some teachers had eight or ten IEP students in their classes, this was a considerable burden, but according to the special education director, "They all do it." These reports were used as part of a discussion that the special education teachers held individually with every IEP student and their family four times each year.

COTEACHING

The second model of special education at Tyler High School was coteaching, which is essentially instruction by general education and special education teachers working collaboratively in the same classroom. Coteaching served students with disabilities in ninth- and tenth-grade language arts. Coteaching also took place in math until the state department of education mandated intensive reading and math classes for students who failed the state standardized test. This mandate made it impossible to stretch the special education staff both to coteach and do the required classes as well.

The coteaching pairs at Tyler High School have been together for several years and have developed relationships that work. One teacher said, "To coteach successfully, you have to really respect each other's methods and get as close to each other as you can if you're going to deal with the kids. In the classroom, we kind of sense and know what the other will be doing and what we need to do. It becomes easy and automatic and that's what it needs to be."

INTENSIVE READING AND MATH

The third model of special education comprised the mandated intensive reading and math courses as supports for students in the ninth grade scoring at a 1 or 2 (less than proficient) on the state's standardized test. Most students with disabilities who were enrolled in intensive reading had both a cotaught reading language arts class and an intensive reading period every day. Similarly, students in intensive math could also take algebra or some other general education course in mathematics. These students get double doses of math and reading every day.

All the intensive classes were taught by special education teachers. The advent of the intensive courses was met with mixed feelings by the special education staff, since staffing these courses meant reducing the number of cotaught classes in English and eliminating coteaching in mathematics entirely.

Given this menu of choices, Carol's mother and the special education director decided that Carol would take a cotaught class in English/Language Arts and be in the mainstream monitoring classes for other subjects. Carol was not a target of the evaluation but Lorraine was outspoken in the family focus groups. She also asked the researchers to watch out for Carol and let her know how Carol was doing in mainstream classes.

It was heartwarming to report that Carol was observed taking an active role in a small-group discussion in science and giggling with a group of her friends on the way to lunch, just another ninth-grade girl. That brought tears to her mother's eyes and that's when she called the special education teachers her "good angels."

Three students with disabilities were Shadowed at Tyler. They were all enrolled in some version of special education. Each of them thrived in the classes chosen for them.

SHADOWING MELISSA

Melissa was a tenth-grader at Tyler High School and on an IEP because of a reading disability. She was the oldest of three children. Her mother said that Melissa never had much use for school until she got to Tyler. Now, her whole attitude has changed and she "stands up straighter."

The special educators kept her mother completely informed about what was going on with Melissa in school. "It's amazing. They call me. I don't have to call them. I always tell them they are a blessing."

On the day she was Shadowed, Melissa's first class was integrated science. The teacher said to the observer, "You can teach anything you want in integrated science" and added that the students believe it's a "low course" because you are assigned to it by reading level. Students who are more advanced in reading were eligible to take physics, biology, or chemistry.

This class had many minority students and, as a minority himself, it depressed the teacher that he believed his students "want everything on a silver platter." He warned them to be careful "not to fall into their own stereotype."

He made it clear that the comment did not apply to Melissa, who was a hard worker. This class was all reading and taking notes on the day she was Shadowed, but Melissa said it was a class she liked and that it was not always bookwork. Last week they got to "make their own electric current."

Melissa's next class was a cotaught English class. The unit was *A Midsummer Night's Dream*. Students were seated in groups of four at tables around the room, and Melissa was in a group with three other girls. The directions for completing the assignment were on the overhead:

- Answer Act II questions.
- Choose a clever name for your group.
- Choose a director/recorder.
- Put the name of your group on a folder.

Even though the special education teacher who was leading this activity provided examples of clever group names, Melissa's group could not think of a name, so they worked individually on the Act II questions. Suddenly, Melissa looked up and suggested the name *Sweet Athenian Ladies* for the group. The others liked the name and began to talk about developing their group project.

Melissa took a leadership role. When the teacher stopped by the table to find out what type of final project they had in mind, Melissa told her that they would probably do a CD cover or a poster.

The first class of the day with no special education support for Melissa was geometry. The topic was area and volume. To make geometry more accessible to special education students, the geometry teacher made and gave the students his own handwritten handouts, which replaced the notes that students usually took themselves.

He explained that by doing notes for the students, he made sure the key points were covered correctly. The first handout contained a calendar and schedule of upcoming tests as well as some problems concerning angles in a triangle. Melissa was quiet throughout the class, but the teacher said that she was a good math student, maintaining a B average without special education support.

The first lesson after lunch for Melissa was intensive reading, a class for students who had less-than-proficient scores on the state test. From several doors away from the classroom, students could be heard laughing. This was not usually the atmosphere in remedial classes at the high-school level, but this was by no means a typical class.

The teacher welcomed the observer and said, "I want you to meet some of my favorite people." The fifteen students waved or said hello and welcome. Melissa seemed a little confused by all this attention and quietly took her seat.

As the teacher read aloud, the students took notes because they were learning to write down the essentials of a story. Often, the teacher stopped reading and asked questions, eliciting students' opinions about the story, which almost all students volunteered to answer.

A popular portion of the lesson was The Word of the Day. This package used cartoons on the overhead and silly little devices, especially puns, to help students learn and retain the words.

The word of the day was "muster." On the overhead was a cartoon in which a bunch of mustard jars stood in military formation. The sentence was, "Each morning, the MUSTARD troops are MUSTERED for roll call." The students loved it, but you have to wonder how often in life they will need to use the word "muster."

The class was reading the novel *The Winning Season* with students reading all the parts aloud. Some assumed British or Southern accents, which the others found hilarious. As Reeny, Melissa read her part slowly but without error.

This class had high energy and everyone, including the teacher, seemed to be having a wonderful time. Later in the day, the observer complimented the teacher and her students on their acting skills and energy.

The next afternoon, there was a laboriously handwritten invitation from the students inviting the observer to visit again, so she could hear them reading the next chapter. Such an invitation must be honored, and the students did an even better job when the observer visited the next day.

Melissa's last class of the day was history with her second minority teacher of the day. As soon as the class settled, the teacher turned on the overhead projector and pointed to handwritten notes. He told the students that the notes contained "basically everything you'll need for your test tomorrow."

He added that anything other than the notes on the overhead was wrong. The overhead notes contained terms such as "imperialism" as well as names and facts. He reviewed some of the terms from his handwritten notes, defining "arbitration" in terms of baseball. This was basically the same technique used by the geometry teacher and may be one of the instructional approaches suggested by special education teachers to make instruction accessible to a range of students.

The teacher explained his reasons for giving notes to students, enumerating them on his fingers:

- His notes are easier to follow than the book.
- He can incorporate materials from many books and other sources.
- There are a lot of student absences and his handouts helped students catch up.
- Many of the students have not learned how to take their own notes.

After about fifteen minutes of note copying, the teacher announced he would let the students pick out of a hat the type of test they would get tomorrow. This raised incredible excitement as the class all rooted for True or False. Sadly, the student selected to do the picking came up with "Short Answer," the type of test they hated most. This was greeted with such groans that the teacher gave into their pleas and made it a word-matching test, which was not as good, according to the students, as True or False, but apparently not as bad as short-answer questions.

Some students grew restless as the class went on and a worksheet followed the note taking, but Melissa never stopped working. In fact, Melissa was never off task all day, although she only became animated in her cotaught English class and her intensive class in reading, both taught by special education teachers.

SHADOWING SERENA

When you first see Serena, you think immediately of Snow White. Serena was then seventeen years old, with jet black hair, smooth, porcelain skin, and deep blue eyes. Drawing closer, you realized she was not Snow White, but rather Sleeping Beauty. Her face held no expression and her eyes lacked focus and spark; a beautiful face, but a blank one.

Serena was not the type of student who was usually Shadowed, but she represented the minority of special education students who spend all their time separately from the general population of the school. What was life like for Serena and other students like her who lived within the school and yet were not part of it?

The resource suite at Van Buren High School was a set of connected rooms at the back of the first floor of the building with two classrooms, a small library area, and its own kitchen. Other students came and went from the resource room, but Serena stayed there all morning until she took one class called "Social and Personal Skills" in another classroom. The other students in that class also had disabilities, so Serena never interacted with the general education students at all.

Serena was a ward of the state and lived in a state-supported group home. Staff from the home brought her to Van Buren the previous spring after she had been rejected by several other area high schools that did not have the resources to serve a student with such severe disabilities.

Unless Van Buren accepted her, it was unlikely that Serena would have gone to school at all. The special education staff said they were horrified by that prospect and worked out an agreement that Serena would attend Van Buren for half a day each day. The group home van would drop her off at the beginning of school and pick her up at noon.

Serena's past was not documented beyond basic facts. Her mother had abandoned the family at some point and Serena's father had turned her over to the state because he was a long-haul truck driver and said he could not care for her.

Doctors suspected that Serena's learning disabilities were due in part to severe early childhood malnutrition. She was having dental work done during the period that she was Shadowed. Her teeth were in very bad shape, neglected in her childhood, the decay exacerbated by her continued devotion to junk food.

Based on his physical examination and Serena's tendency to be a "cutter," the doctor who examined her also suspected sexual abuse. She could not be trusted with anything sharp, even a paper clip, or she would start scratching at her arms and legs.

Serena was late for school the first day of Shadowing and the teachers asked that the observer not attempt to engage her in conversation because she was so easily distracted. That seemed odd since in a small room, Serena would probably notice she was the focus of an observation. The teachers said, "No, Serena doesn't notice much beyond her immediate environment and we're still not sure how much of that she comprehends."

These two veteran special education teachers, who spent their days just as separated from the mainstream of the school as the students they taught, managed some of the most difficult students in the school. They did so with grace, good humor, and a positive attitude.

They were not just providing a respite from the group home for Serena, they were determined to equip her to protect herself in the outside world. "She is so beautiful and so innocent," one of the teachers said, "that we shudder to think what could happen to her."

They hoped to keep Serena in school until she was twenty-one and gradually, as she learned social skills, bring her into general education classrooms. If all went well, Serena would receive a certificate of completion in lieu of a regular diploma, which might enable her to live independently and find work of some kind.

The first class on the day she was Shadowed was "Life Skills Management" and the topic was "Taking Medications Safely." In addition to Serena, who was escorted into the room about ten minutes late, there were nine other students in the class and the teachers led a lively and interesting class discussion about medications. A pharmacy could be stocked with the medications these students were taking, or their parents were taking or, in one case, the family dog was taking.

It would have been a useful discussion for Serena, who was on several major medications, but she didn't participate. It was not clear if she realized the relevance of the topic to herself or if she really understood the conversation. Serena's face gave nothing away.

Throughout the class, Serena played with her binder. The binder was apparently Serena's most prized personal possession, or possibly her only one. It was a dark red canvas notebook that zipped around three sides. Inside, on the right was a stack of blank three-hole lined paper and on the left a pocket with a calculator and several smaller pockets, each holding a pen or pencil.

Serena zipped and unzipped that binder over and over every day she was Shadowed. Each time, she would examine everything in it, and then zip the binder up again. She never used things from the binder. Her satisfaction seemed to derive from knowing everything was present and accounted for.

Serena's second class was "Life Skills Reading" with a substitute teacher that day. Serena did nothing in the class unless you count zipping and unzipping the binder as an activity. The next day, her regular teacher said that focusing and refocusing Serena on school work was a daily challenge, but she had found some learning activities to engage her interest.

Serena loved maps. She would spend a long time finding New Mexico, the last place from which she had received a letter from her mother. She had traced a route to New Mexico, marking it with a red pen.

The teacher was building on this interest by helping Serena start a scrapbook of pictures and articles about New Mexico. She had tears in her eyes as she described Serena's enthusiasm for this project, "Sometimes I think there is a real mind in there, struggling to get out."

"Social and Personal Skills" was taught by a special education teacher, but located in a large, airy upstairs classroom, a nice break from the resource suite. An aide escorted Serena upstairs, and explained she was not allowed to go anywhere in the school by herself, because she might wander away.

Serena paid no attention to the conversation, although she could obviously hear it. She also did not notice the other students, nor they her. She resembled some beautiful fairy tale princess who was under an evil spell of invisibility.

The "Social and Personal Skills" class comprised Serena and five boys, who had been diagnosed with severe anger-management issues. There was also a teacher, and a brawny male aide who was there in case of discipline issues. The teacher began the class by requesting that students write their personal goals for this week and next week.

The teacher asked: "What if I set a goal and don't meet it?" Serena, who momentarily looked animated replied, "failure, not succeeding." The teacher nodded and asked, "What are some typical responses to failure?" The other students contributed things like "anger," "acting out," "frustration," but Serena had lost interest and left her seat to stare out the window.

When the teacher asked, "What happens when you feel helpless?" Serena responded immediately, "suicide, turning to drugs, self-abuse." The teacher said that when people have feelings like that, they respond in many destructive ways.

She gave examples and Serena returned to her seat, interested again. When the teacher described a boy with bad behavior Serena said, "He's showing anger." Perhaps, Serena's life had included therapy at some point and she was repeating things she remembered from that experience.

Near the end of the class, as a reward for her good participation, the teacher gave Serena candy to hand out to the other students. She walked around the room, letting the students reach into the bag and take a handful. When she reached a boy, who had exhibited discipline problems during the class and now had his head down on his desk, Serena stood and regarded him as if thinking what she should do and then shook her head and did not offer him candy.

This seemed to be a sign of cognition and perception in Serena. She recognized her classmate's feelings and reacted appropriately. A boy who had been physically restrained about five minutes ago was probably not in the mood for candy. Even as an observer, you could not help but look for positive signs in Serena's behavior. Everyone wanted so much for her to get better.

When class ended, it was lunchtime and the aide was at the door to escort Serena to the office where the van driver picked her up to go back to the group home. She actually said a few words to the guard at the front door and smiled at him, the first smile of the day.

On our second visit to Van Buren, the first sight of Serena was in the kitchen of the resource suite, where her two special education teachers were showing her how to make a salad and explaining why it was important to eat nourishing food. All three wore aprons around their waists. It was a family scene; the little kitchen, two loving aunts, and an attentive young niece.

Serena looked better than she had in the fall. Her hair was glossier and new white dentures sparkled in her mouth. It was hard to tell if she was engaged in the salad making process or just enjoying the attention, but she smiled and nodded as the teachers talked to her.

This visit featured the Kids with Cameras activity with all the Shadowed students. Although others were dubious that Serena would understand the challenge well enough to participate, one of her teachers said it would be a good experience for her. The teacher and Serena were seen all around the school taking pictures that day.

The next morning Serena and her teacher came into the conference room and Serena looked at her pictures and explained them softly to her teacher, who then repeated the information to the observer. It was like interviewing someone who spoke another language and needed a translator, but as the teacher explained the pictures, Serena watched closely and often nodded her approval.

The first six pictures taken by Serena were all of a man wearing a uniform and an embarrassed expression. "That is Mr. Kaminski. He is the security guard. He keeps us safe." Then came three pictures of a woman in uniform, also looking embarrassed. "She is the police officer. She keeps us safe too." The other pictures were all of her teachers. That small world was high school for Serena.

The following fall, one of Serena's teachers met the research team at the front door. "We have lost her," she said. Just two weeks before, Serena's father had arrived to claim her. He was remarried and said he had a home for Serena in a trailer park hundreds of miles away. Serena had now turned eighteen, and her teachers suspected that he was more interested in Serena's social security disability check than in her well-being.

The teachers asked him to wait while the office prepared Serena's transcript, so she could attend school in another district. Her father said he was in a hurry and would send for it later. He did not do so. One of the teachers tried to track Serena, so she could notify the local school authorities and possibly get her back to school but she was not successful.

And so, a badly damaged young girl was lost and found and then lost again. Do such things really happen? Yes, they do, and that's why even special education angels weep sometimes.

Families, even the students themselves, may perceive placement in special education as the sound of a door closing. How can they face the prospect of their children living forever sequestered from the regular kids and a normal life? But when the staff of a school like Tyler recognizes the capability instead of the challenges faced by students with disabilities, you find that special education is really the sound of a door opening.

Chapter 8

Who Destroyed Coteaching at Hanover Middle School?

The story of coteaching at Hanover Middle School is a cautionary tale about the fragility of school reform and innovation. A research-based program was adopted, implemented, and continued briefly at Hanover. However, research warns that schools and districts are social systems and decisions can be made to reject programs, even after they are fully integrated into the system. So it was at Hanover Middle School.

EVOLUTION OF A VISIONARY SCHOOL

The Cedar County School District needed to build a new middle school to meet the county's growing student population. The principal, Dr. Florio, and his administrative staff wanted Hanover Middle School to embody the most effective practices and knowledge that research could offer. They formed a study group with the goal of inventing a school with the best possible integration of philosophies and practices for their student population, which included a high percentage of families living in poverty, migrant families, and students with disabilities.

Hanover Middle School would serve the children of people who worked in the tourist hotels, cleaned for the affluent families who lived in the area, and provided the restaurants with kitchen help. It would be the only high-poverty middle school in the district and the only one serving families whose first language was not English.

Their mission statement became "Access to rigorous curriculum through schoolwide inclusive practices." They then proceeded to determine the key ideas that would shape the school:

- Students learn when they have a sense of safety and personal connection.
- Students learn when instruction is responsive to multiple intelligences and individual learning styles.
- Adults need to collaborate to create a personalized and academically rigorous learning community.

The study group decided that placing general and special education teachers together in coteaching teams would help all students to learn in an active and challenging environment and would turn their vision of the school into a coherent schoolwide approach.

Dr. Florio involved his teachers in thinking through various coteaching models. In search of the most effective approach, coteaching went through three incarnations over a three-year period: (1) a collaborative model; (2) a traveling teacher mode; and (3) a schoolwide model.

The Collaborative Model. Implementing the collaborative model entailed setting up a number of inclusion classrooms with ten general education students, ten special education students, and two teachers, one a general education teacher and the other a special education teacher.

Each inclusion class was a self-contained unit without any specific contact with other teachers and classrooms. The drawback, in the eyes of the principal and the study group, was that this coteaching model was isolated. The only teachers who had to think about teaching students with disabilities were those that taught the inclusion classes.

The Traveling Teacher Model. The next model consisted of special education teachers who "traveled," following a cohort of students with disabilities from one classroom to another to provide services in different subjects. Again, the administrators saw deficiencies in the model. The special education teacher focused solely on the needs of the students with disabilities who were placed in a classroom. She did not participate in planning the lesson for the whole class and might or might not have access to the lesson plan for the day. Often, she was left to wing it, despite good intentions on both sides.

In the Traveling Teacher model, the special education teachers were all on one team, which spanned grade levels. They met separately to discuss issues and students within the realm of special education instruction. They were not part of the general education teams—comprised of the English/language arts teacher, a math teacher, a science teacher, and a social studies teacher.

The Schoolwide Model. The schoolwide coteaching model placed students with disabilities in heterogeneous classrooms with the special education teacher now a core team member. To introduce the model, Dr. Florio sent some special education teachers to visit other middle schools around the state that were also experimenting with teaming special education and general education teachers in classrooms.

One of the special education teachers said, "The first year I began in a self-contained classroom—toward the end of the year I was approached about joining the sixth-grade team. It would be the first time that we really tried a true team concept with an inclusion model. Dr. Florio gave us the chance to create something incredible."

This model made the status of special education teachers equal to that of the subject area teachers and created an interdisciplinary team. Coteaching became the expression of interdisciplinary teaming in the classroom. It created a marriage of the general education teachers' content knowledge and the special education teachers' strategies for making that content accessible to all students.

The special education teachers carved out their own niche in the teams, drawing on their expertise in understanding and responding to students' and teachers' needs. A special education teacher described her challenging role in the cotaught classroom: "In an inclusion or coteaching model, we have to consider not only our students' needs, but also the regular education teachers' needs. We're entering their environment and we have to be the ones to go one step above and beyond. I'm the bridge between the students and the services that they need."

The schoolwide model called for the special education teacher to plan with the entire team and then teach with each teacher on the team for some part of the week. At a minimum, the special education teacher had three roles:

- Served as a subject matter teacher in classrooms that included students with disabilities;
- Understood these students' learning strengths and needs; and
- Modeled, for the content teacher, ways to make complex content accessible.

The collaboration met with some initial resistance, especially from general education teachers who didn't like the notion of sharing their classroom with another coequal teacher. The assistant principal dealt with this potential stumbling block by using what he called "tough love."

"I paired them up and then I put each pair in an empty classroom and told them not to come out until they had worked out the parameters of a partnership. They all did and it went smoothly after that. We began to see the buy-in of regular education teachers when they realized that this was not only benefiting special education students, but also benefiting every student in the school."

The schoolwide model became an effective and valued component at Hanover and it seemed permanently embedded in the life of the school. When observing in a cotaught classroom at Hanover Middle School, you might see instruction around a math concept such as measuring the radius and circumference of a circle. The general education teacher stood at the front of the class explaining the meaning of the terms, while the special education teacher stood at a blackboard at the side of the room, illustrating the concepts with diagrams.

The students listened to the teacher at the front of the room and then swiveled their heads to look at the diagrams. The experience was both visual and auditory and it was obvious that the two teachers had planned the lesson cooperatively. When a student asked a question, either teacher might answer or one might build on the other's response.

A SLOW UNRAVELING

In the third year of implementation of the schoolwide model, some small clouds appeared on the horizon. They came from several sources, primarily from policy decisions made by the district that affected staffing and later the very existence of coteaching at Hanover Middle School.

Teacher Turnover. During the implementation process, Hanover had benefited from an influx of young, energetic teachers. As a rapidly growing district, Cedar County recruited large numbers of new teachers each year.

In order to staff the few nonaffluent schools in the district, many new teachers were placed at Hanover Middle School every year. To ensure some stability, the teachers were compelled to stay at Hanover for three years before they could request a transfer.

At the end of their three-year contracts, almost all the teachers moved on to schools with fewer challenges and higher salaries. In those three years, the school experienced an 80 percent turnover in staff. Three years later, only one classroom teacher who had experienced the success of coteaching remained at the school.

District Interference. Because of its stellar reputation as a school that accommodated students with disabilities, the district opted to create a center for severely emotionally disabled students at Hanover Middle School. The school thus became the home for all severely emotionally disturbed students across the district.

District administrators ignored the resistance of Hanover Middle School administrators to this wholesale change in the composition of their school. The district placed these new students in self-contained classes taught by teachers who did not expect to play an active role in the larger school. Many students in this population suffered anger-management issues and would occasionally act out.

Keeping the center in a separate wing of the school was a measure to protect other students and teachers. The center also absorbed administrator time to deal with discipline and behavior issues and seemed to affect school climate negatively. One wing of the building was part of the school, but not part of the school community.

Changing Student Population. At the same time as a nearby town acquired a charter school, which attracted most of Hanover's affluent students, a new population of English as a Second Language (ESL) and migrant families moved into the area. Continuing to embed coteaching within interdisciplinary teams became a greater challenge as the composition of the school's population changed and outside sources of funding provided by special grants dried up.

School District Relationship. The district had no part in the design of the coteaching model and therefore no stake in it. Rather than attempting to enlist district support for the coteaching process, Dr. Florio put his efforts toward "flying below the radar," which enabled him to institute changes without drawing district's attention to them.

This gave him leeway to create and implement his design, but he built no advocacy base for it outside the school. The district, which had neither helped nor hindered the creation of the reform, also neither helped nor hindered its demise.

Although the Hanover Middle School coteaching model gained national recognition and visitors came from all over the state and region to observe in the cotaught classrooms, Hanover never enjoyed active district support for its inclusive approach to special education. As one district administrator noted, "There are two kinds of schools that make districts nervous, those that lag way behind and those that are way ahead of the curve. Hanover makes people very nervous." Schools that take individual actions that go beyond the norms of the district make administrators feel that they are losing control.

Leadership Change. When Dr. Florio left the school, the system suffered what seemed only a minor worry, since the new principal was promoted from Hanover Elementary School and was considered to be part of the school family. She was already experienced with the schoolwide model of inclusion. Also, the assistant principal, a major architect of the coteaching model remained in place.

It turned out, however, that the new principal had her own priorities. When she received a large federal grant in her first year, the faculty expected that the new funds would support the continuation of the schoolwide co-teaching model.

The principal instead wished to use the funding to include the ESL students in the general education classrooms. Until then, the ESL students had been placed on their own separate team. Classrooms were now inclusive of both students with disabilities and students who spoke very little English.

To accommodate this change, the principal reverted to the traveling-teacher model of special education support. Special educators were no longer members of interdisciplinary teams but moved from one classroom to another in order to make sure special education students and ESL students received consistent support.

The principal's other priority was to increase teachers' accountability for results. She said, "There was no accountability in the past, now teachers resent my emphasis on it. Every day I'm writing someone up and taking someone to task." The principal zeroed in on a group of teachers she called "the malcontents." She said, "They think I'm picking on them and they try to pull other people into their negativity."

In the middle of her second year, this principal suddenly accepted a job at the district level, leaving Hanover Middle School with no clearly defined model of special education or ESL student inclusion. Teacher morale was low and the principal who replaced her had not worked at the middle-school level previously and had no interest in the inclusion of ESL or special education students.

Principal #3 focused on ability grouping, which is the antithesis of inclusion. He also promised the district dramatic test score improvements, which did not occur. This principal was unable either to improve achievement or boost teacher morale. The fourth principal in five years completed the destruction of the vision that had been the foundation of the Hanover Middle School philosophy.

THE VILLAIN OF THE STORY

The obvious nominee for the role of villain of the Hanover Middle School story was the menace of Unintended Consequences. The district certainly did not intend for Hanover to lose about one-third of its teaching staff every year. It was an unintended consequence of their policy of having new teachers start in struggling schools and not having many struggling schools in which to place them.

In his decision to fly under the radar, Dr. Florio did not realize that he was setting up a scenario in which the district, neither understanding nor appreciating the innovation that was taking place at Hanover Middle School, did not value it. When special grant money no longer helped support the coteaching model, the district did not think highly enough of the practice to provide resources for it.

Hanover Middle School is an extreme example of a set of circumstances that happen over and over again in schools with the most economically disadvantaged and vulnerable students. New teachers, particularly in large urban districts, are often placed in such schools.

The type of placement is not always district policy, but a consequence of frequent teacher turnover in struggling schools. These schools are where the openings occur, and new teachers accept the assignment knowing that as soon as they have established themselves, they can move on.

Often, these same schools are the setting for whole-school reform models, which invest extensive resources in professional development. They spend thousands of dollars instilling knowledge and skills that leave the school when the teachers who have been trained transfer to more stable and affluent schools.

In fact, the real villain here is an overdependence on Tacit Knowledge. Most research on knowledge management comes from the private sector, which appreciates the importance of differentiating Explicit Knowledge, that which is written down and clearly articulated, and Tacit Knowledge, which exists in the mind and in the culture of institutions.

Tacit knowledge includes cultural beliefs, values, attitudes, and models as well as skills, capabilities, and expertise. The "Glossary of Knowledge Management"[1] notes that "tacit knowledge is difficult to articulate, and so it tends to be shared through discussion, stories, and personal interactions." At Hanover Middle School, teacher turnover became a loss of valued tacit knowledge that, because it was undocumented, was also irretrievable.

New teachers who came to the school during the reign of the second and third principals came into an environment altered to accommodate the new leaders' priorities. Their priorities became increasingly contradictory to the spirit of inclusion that was the original vision of the school established by Dr. Florio. He had not built bridges or created advocates for inclusion at the district level.

The teachers who could articulate the vision were gone and little explicit evidence of their work remained. There was no manual or set of videos to show what inclusion looked like when it was done well.

However, one source of support did exist that no one thought to tap into. The families of students with disabilities at Hanover were enthusiastic supporters of the inclusion and coteaching model. When they band together, families can exert great leverage on a school or a school district. Had Dr. Florio founded a group called "Parents for Coteaching at Hanover Middle School" and directed their voices toward the district office, the chances of coteaching surviving would have been enhanced.

NOTE

1. Olivier Serrat, "Glossary of Knowledge Management," *Knowledge Solutions* 39 (April 2009): 3.

Chapter 9

Adult Basic Education

A Program in the Shadows

They say that doctors bury their mistakes and architects plant ivy. The failures and mistakes of education are simply lost in the larger world unless they turn up in Adult Basic Education (ABE) programs, a tremendous resource that is little appreciated.

In an overlooked corner of the education establishment in every state, you will find ABE programs for adults with low reading skills. Broadly speaking, there are three populations in ABE, including: native English-speaking adults who failed in their earlier school experiences; out-of-school youth sixteen years or older; and ESL learners.

Your first encounter with ABE is likely to surprise you, especially if your experience has been within the K–12 system. In ABE, you see such poverty and scarcity of resources. On the other hand, you also see amazingly dedicated teachers and earnest learners. For the students in these programs, they are life-altering opportunities.

All the programs in ABE address literacy issues, but their fundamental missions differ in philosophy and goals. For example, the rather narrow mission of one program focuses entirely on academics. "The goal of this program is to aid adults in understanding the basics of reading, writing, math, and speaking skills." Other programs take a much more inclusive approach. One states that its broad purpose is "Empowering adult learners through the acquisition of basic skills and English language proficiency in order to become responsible, productive, and independent members of society."

THE ABE LEARNERS

The missions of all the ABE programs are valid and important. Nonetheless, the population of adult learners who face many life and learning challenges find that their personal education goals are difficult to achieve.

Native English Speakers. Older adults in ABE programs are likely to be native English speakers who failed in school. They are among the most motivated and often the least skilled learners in ABE programs. Some of them have actually graduated from high school without being able to read. They were passed over from year to year because no one dealt with them.

Many of these adults have managed to conceal illiteracy or confided in only one person, usually a spouse or trusted friend. One hotel housekeeper was unable to read the notes left by guests such as, "Please change the light bulb." For several years she took these notes to her supervisor to read them to her.

These learners may have attended school before the diagnosis of learning disabilities became sophisticated or widespread enough to catch their reading issues. For every one of them, entering into an ABE program is an act of courage since they must overcome their fear of school, the stigma of illiteracy, and the embarrassment of letting others know they cannot read.

Malcolm, for example, had been the janitor at an elementary school for nine years. Only one teacher in the school knew that he could not read. He brought the notes he received from other teachers to her and she read them aloud. If she was absent for some reason, he told everyone he had broken his glasses. He said he lived a life of constant anxiety, fearing he would lose his job if anyone in authority found out that he couldn't read.

Out-of-School Teens. High-school students drop out of school for a variety of reasons, some academic and some personal. ABE program directors may have different views of the motivation of these students. One said, "These kids don't fit into the life of the high school. These are kids with adult responsibilities They may be kids who were abused, have alcoholic parents, or they have a kid of their own. They're not into going to the prom; they just want to get that diploma."

Other program directors see the young learners more cynically. "These young people are laboring under the delusion that a General Equivalency Diploma (GED) is much easier to get than a high school diploma." Actually, the GED or the more recent High School Equivalency Test (HiSET) is more difficult to obtain than a high-school diploma. Many high-school students cannot pass the GED without preparation and assistance.

ESL Learners. Non-English-speaking learners make up an increasing segment of the ABE population. Some may just need to learn the English language, but some also have learning disabilities or did not acquire reading and writing skills in their native countries. Given the language barrier, these issues may not surface until the learner has been in classes for a while.

Minorities are overrepresented in many ABE programs. One director said that Latinos comprise 37 percent of her program, although they represent only 10 percent of the community population. Native Americans are also overrepresented; the population is 5 percent in the community and 11 percent in her program. She believes this is a reflection of the way they were treated in school. "Some teachers don't believe minorities can be successful academically, and it's a self-fulfilling prophecy."

HOW ABE PROGRAMS WORK

The process of enrolling and progressing through a curriculum and some kind of assessment of progress is similar to that of traditional public schools, but in adult education programs, everything is more complex.

Intake. Learners may come into the program with little or no documentation of their prior education experience. Every program has an intake specialist who administers specialized assessments and assigns the new learners to a level in the program based on their results.

Intake interviews are also important in identifying oral skills and learning disabilities. Intake specialists usually have a standard set of questions that helps to uncover learning disabilities. For example:

- Have you ever been in special education classes?
- Can you memorize the multiplication tables?
- Do any family members have learning disabilities?
- Do you often forget how to spell words you know?

Individual programs define reading levels differently. The lowest level may include nonreaders through grade 6 or 7, or programs may define first-level learners as those whose reading competency is below the sixth grade. Everyone else is pre-GED or more currently HiSET in some states. Still others define first-level readers as those whose reading skills are below the third-grade level.

Goals. An important component of the intake process is setting personal goals with each learner. Some learners set modest goals such as, "I want to be able to read to my children" but many, regardless of reading level, say that the reason they are there is to get their GED or HiSET. In many states, a high-school diploma or a high-school equivalency diploma is required before people can seek gainful employment.

One program specialist never tells the learners that their goals are unrealistic. She encourages learners, no matter what level they start at, to think in terms of an entire education that continues on through the community college level. To encourage the learners to think long term, a career counselor and employment counselor are available to low-level learners. The career counselor works with people at all stages in the learning process to find out what their interests are, what their images are of the future, and how they are setting goals to get there.

Another intake specialist considers that part of the process involves setting realistic goals. These goals are based on what the learner "really wants to do" and she helps each learner to set short-term and long-term goals. If the goals are unrealistic, according to the counselor, it's usually because the learner does not understand what a realistic goal is and through discussion, they are able to come to consensus.

Instructors. The salaries for instructors in adult education are abysmally low. Most are part-time, hourly employees. If they work for a community college, they are adjunct faculty, ineligible for benefits or tenure. In one program, the director said, "Many are here because they didn't find a full-time job or because their personal status changed, for example, their children entered school and they feel less need to be home with them."

Salaries are so low in one program that the director looked for people who she felt would do a good job even if their backgrounds were not in education. The formal qualifications for her program are a bachelor's degree or experience in adult education.

A new director of another program wanted to give the teachers respect by paying them a decent salary. She went to the board to get approval for hiring a lead teacher at a salary of $30,000 a year. The board wanted to pay $23,000 and the director took a stand. She said that she would not even advertise for the position at that salary. She prevailed.

Volunteers. Volunteers, especially volunteer tutors, have been the backbone of ABE from the beginning. A recurring issue in the past was that some volunteer tutors treated the learners as children who did not know how to budget, shop, or make important life decisions. The learners, despite their handicaps, are adults and they resented the intrusion into their lives.

As adult education has become more professionalized, the training of tutors has improved and there is more oversight of their work. One program director uses tutors in the classrooms, where they can work with individuals or small groups, thereby allowing more individualization of instruction within the classroom format. She prefers this because tutors are working closely with a certified teacher and the program maintains more control over their work.

In another program in which volunteers work with the lower-level students one-on-one, the staff keeps individual learner folders updated daily so a student and tutor need only open the folder to see what they are supposed to be doing. One tutor who has no background in teaching reading is completely comfortable because "The students bring the papers they are working on and the sessions always follow the same routine of reading, comprehending, and answering questions."

It is still common practice for volunteer tutors to work individually with learners whose skills are so low that they cannot function in a class. However, one program director strongly disagrees with the practice. "We have tutors serving nonreaders. We are using the least qualified instructors for the learners most in need. This is not a recipe for success. These learners need every tool."

Location. Programs may be administered by the state K–12 division or by the postsecondary division. If the ABE program is sponsored by a local community college, as is often the case, they may offer some classes at the college and then set up various satellite locations in the neighborhoods where the learners are likely to live.

Donated sites are used whenever possible. For example, one evening ABE class was held in the basement of a church, which was cramped, dark, dingy, and so cold that everybody kept their coats on. The instructors said, "We don't meet here for the ambiance. We meet here because it's free." Since the room is used for other meetings, this instructor must carry all his materials in and out of the building twice a week, including a portable white board and a laptop computer.

A very large community college program has twenty-three program sites that offer ABE. The main one is located in a building that used to be a grocery store. It is in a decayed inner-city neighborhood of small stores and fast-food restaurants. An instructor noted that the staff and volunteers must have cars, because taxis refuse to pick up or drop off passengers in the neighborhood.

Attendance. Students' varied life circumstances and personal challenges hamper their attendance. Challenges are rampant, such as not having bus fare to get to class, child health issues, child care issues, work schedules, and domestic abuse. Many have medical problems and suffer from depression or anxiety. Also, some learners lack initial motivation because they are required to be in the program by a judge, perhaps as a condition of parole. Once enrolled in the program, they usually see its benefits.

Except when life issues get in the way, attendance at ABE programs is generally very high. Some learners make progress very slowly but they attend class sessions faithfully. An instructor says. "It is a place to go. They have friends here. It's not just about learning."

One program offers student-support meetings, in which learners get together on a monthly basis and encourage each other. These meetings, according to the intake specialist, "are surprisingly successful" with an average attendance of eight to ten students. The students get to talk to others who have similar learning disabilities. They may request a speaker from a bank or newspaper. They may bring in photos and talk about them.

Interpersonal Skills. Discipline issues are rare in ABE classes, but one social worker reported that a teacher sometimes invited her to work on an issue of classroom dynamics. She said that the learners have a lot of inter-action with their teachers and "they take everything so personally, that situations can arise." Many students have such low interpersonal skills that they interrupt and contradict the teacher. Or, a few dominant personalities may create a bad atmosphere in the class.

The issue of interpersonal skills among low-level learners was highlighted by a program of round table discussions sponsored by a large charitable foundation. The premise underlying the program was that low-level learners, although they may lack reading and writing skills, have adult opinions on issues such as immigration, legalizing marijuana, and birth control. The point of the program was to engage the participants in adult discussion.

The program didn't work well, not because the learners did not have opinions, but because they lacked the vocabulary to discuss any issue object-ively. On one side were the people who only knew how to speak belligerently ("That's what I think and nobody's going to change my mind"). On the other side were those learners who only knew how to be subservient, agreeing with every opinion expressed, even if the opinions were diametrically opposed.

Curriculum and Instruction. The approach to instruction differs by program, but two approaches dominate. One is the use of a packaged curric-ulum that provides materials, assessments, and class assignments. Teachers have to attend intense training to become certified to offer the curriculum, but many think it is worth it to have a complete instructional package.

Other program directors and instructors like to build on the learners' life experience and create curriculum around them. In one daily ABE program, the television set is tuned to the news and each learner has a newspaper sub-scription. The first fifteen minutes is devoted to silent reading of the paper and watching whatever news is being presented on the TV screen.

A brief discussion of the news showed once again that the learners experienced difficulty with their conversational skills. The volunteer tutors took turns contributing their opinions and modeling the idea of give and take in discussion. An instructor said that even though the discussions can get "gnarly," the learners are gaining an important skill.

In this program, the first structured activity was called reading/thinking. It began with learners taking turns to read aloud, and then they broke into small groups to answer questions. On the day of observation, they read a brief piece about someone trying to get her apartment cleaned up after she heard that company was coming in two hours. The small groups worked to address these issues: What are you most worried about? Is it being embarrassed or feeding your guests? Decide what would you do about that and write out your step-by-step plan.

The instructor assigned roles such as recorder, timekeeper, and reporter, and the groups reported back after working for about ten minutes. The groups were notable for the intensity with which they tackled the questions and attempted to devise the step-by-step plan. While the original piece was some-what humorous, the learners took it all seriously.

In some ABE programs, a packaged curriculum is used in tandem with teacher-developed instruction. For example, one instructor believed that the packaged program she used in the morning did not convey the pleasure of reading. For their afternoon session, she attempted to find high-interest, low-level vocabulary reading books.

The very first session with that group was an outing to the library to make sure every learner had a library card and knew how to use it. For many of the learners, it was the first time they had ever set foot in a public library, but the cards became a point of pride.

The director of one program added a civics class for the ESL students after 9/11. The class focused on the government and culture of the United States. Students were taken on a tour of the courthouse, found out where all the public schools and the police station were located, and learned the details of the various systems that they needed to understand.

Assessment. As in so many areas of education, the standardized assessment of learner achievement has become more important in ABE. Progress is harder to measure than in the K–12 system because of the prevalence of undiagnosed learning disabilities and the slow pace of achievement among many adults. One intake specialist's informal assessment is that 95 percent of low-level learners in their program have some kind of learning disability.

A program director said he must report progress to the state on a monthly basis. Progress in this program was defined as improved performance in academic classes, good attendance, and how well the student is doing in the computer class. Progress also included results on tests, which are given to students each time they complete fifty hours of attendance.

An instructor of students with very low reading scores believed that more than a third of her students had learning disabilities, many of them quite severe. It was a challenge for them to demonstrate enough progress to stay in the program, and yet they were the students who attended most faithfully and the instructor believed that they were the students who needed "to be here" in order to have some positive structure in their lives.

Thus, while the movement of learners from one level to another is quite systematic, one instructor juggles the books with the students within her class. She does this openly and because she believes it is right. She gave the example of a grandmother whose only goal was to read to her grand-children. In terms of programmatic assessment, the grandmother made very little progress, but the instructor kept her in the program until she could read *Goodnight Moon* fluently.

The reason that instructors want to retain as many learners as possible in their programs as long as they want to attend is that the ABE programs are the last stop for many people who have not learned to read. It also offers a better life for teens who have dropped out of school and it is the gateway to citizenship for the ESL population.

Section Three

SCHOOLS IN NEED

Chapter 10

Failing Schools, Faulty Solutions

Researchers can generate a mental portrait of a failing school just by reviewing its published data from the previous three years. Standardized test scores are stagnant or falling, and the gap between the highest-achieving students and the lowest has widened as some students fall further and further behind.

In failing schools, teacher turnover is high, as is teacher absenteeism. The school has a high rate of student suspensions and two or possibly three principals have come and gone in the three-year period. There is widespread eligibility among the students for free or reduced lunch.

The most common remedy offered for failing schools is the creation of charter schools. That succeeds in moving students around but not necessarily in improving their education.

INSIDE A FAILING SCHOOL

One visit to a failing school brings the picture into sharp and shocking focus. The first clue arises when a visitor pushes the buzzer at the entrance to gain admittance. Someone in the office is supposed to answer the buzz, ask the identity of the visitor through the intercom, and then unlock the door.

The visitor pushes the button again and again and peers into the reinforced glass of the door. Finally, a passing teacher or student opens the door, never inquiring who is visiting or why.

Inside the school, crumpled papers lie on the floor and there are posters on the bulletin board for events that took place six months ago. Broken desks or chairs are left in the hallways like abandoned victims of violence.

The Naysayers. A set of skeptical veteran teachers often becomes the de facto leaders of failing schools. This group comprises teachers who have stayed at the school over many years because of inertia or because they haven't been recruited elsewhere. They bond with similar teachers and become the naysayers, automatically resisting every new approach, idea, and program.

These teachers gain power through longevity while principals and other teachers come and go. When a new program is introduced, they say, "We tried that ten years ago and it didn't work" or "That would never work with *my* students" as if their students came from some faraway, unfriendly planet. The naysayers resist any change, because the school works well for them just the way it is.

At one school involved in a research study, the new principal who encountered a cadre of naysayers decided that the only approach to the problem was "crashing their party" by making sure the naysaying teachers followed every school rule to the letter. He took attendance at meetings that the naysayers had previously not bothered to attend. He insisted on seeing lesson plans every day, a custom they had not followed for several years.

The principal frequently checked their classrooms to make sure that a goal for each lesson was posted on the board. The following September, he greeted the researchers swinging an imaginary bat. "Five retirements and every one of them a home run."

Lack of Cleanliness. A failing school is often dirty, with slovenly house-keeping apparent in dead plants and dusty drapes. Some teachers will say that students don't notice their surroundings, but of course they do. At one such school, five seventh-graders came to participate in a focus group. Delilah stopped inside the door of the conference room where the group was to meet and wrinkled her nose in disgust as she looked around the room.

At one point in the discussion, the students were asked what change would make the school a better place for them, and that was Delilah's cue. "Look at this room," she said. "If you shake the curtains, you get like a hundred years of dust and there are dead flies on the window sill. This table is even sticky." Four other students tested the table with their forefingers and nodded in solemn agreement. The table really was sticky.

Delilah was not just a complainer. She had a solution and soon she had all of the other students excitedly taking part. She wanted to write to one of the home improvement shows on cable TV and ask for a makeover. "They could do it in one weekend and our parents could help and we could all be on TV." That did it. She now had five proponents of a makeover.

When the idea reached the ears of the principal, she put the kibosh on it instantly. It would be "bad publicity for the school and district and it was not necessary." The first statement may have been true; the second was not.

Actually, it was necessary. For many hours a day, the school was home to the students and the teachers. If the principal was willing to spearhead the effort, if she brought the teachers, families, and students together to give the school a deep cleaning, the work would have been rewarded with an improved sense of community and higher morale.

Discipline. It is counterintuitive, but failing schools are likely to be very quiet, the silence representing strict discipline. In happier schools, there is a continuous buzz, like bees around the hive, of students and teachers talking and working together. Principals of failing schools are proud of the quiet, orderly hallways and silent classrooms full of students sitting at rows of desks, listening to the teacher who is doing all the talking.

Achieving such control may come at a price. Harsh discipline, even physical discipline, is acceptable in some schools and some states. Mr. Miller was the dean of discipline in a large high school in a major city. In response to routine questions about ways of dealing with student behavior he said, "I offer the kids a choice, either detention after school or I can paddle them." He added, "You'd be surprised; most of them come in here and say, 'Hit me Mr. Miller.' That's what they really prefer."

That statement seemed so unlikely that it became the topic of a student focus group later in the day. Was it true they chose paddling over detention? Two of the seven in the group, a boy and a girl, admitted they had in fact done so. The girl mumbled that it was "too embarrassing to talk about" and lowered her eyes.

The boy explained that he had an afterschool job and his family depended on the money he earned. He could not afford to be late to work, so he chose paddling. "He leans you over one of the desks and he hits your backside with this wooden paddle. It's not so bad. He doesn't hit that hard." The girl looked up with tears in her eyes and said, "Yes, it is; it's horrible. I wanted to die when it happened to me."

The students could have told their families, but they feared that Mr. Miller would retaliate somehow. They could have told the principal, but they assumed he already knew and condoned the practice. So, they suffered in silence.

Bullying Teachers. Teachers sometimes become so embittered that they begin to bully students, often choosing a target that is likely to react and who can then be punished. Mr. Bessler was a social studies teacher in a middle school where Nick was a ninth-grade student with anger-management issues. When the bell rang to begin class, Mr. Bessler took attendance.

When he reached Nick's name, Mr. Bessler suddenly bellowed, "Mr. Mathews. I'm glad you decided to grace us with your presence today. I find your absences to be excessive. You need to make up work. Your grade is down. You know, guy, you never made up the work from when you were absent. I keep track of 140 kids, Nick. I can't spend time keeping track of you. Isn't that right Mr. Matthews?"

Nick, his head down, his face red, replied politely enough, "Stop yelling at me." The teacher said "I'm not yelling at you." But he was. "I just care what happens to you. You won't be able to get away with this in high school." In an interview later in the day, Nick said mildly, "Well, he is basically right. I do have trouble getting stuff made up. I was out sick for a week and I missed a lot of work."

In subsequent days, Nick managed to contain his anger, as Mr. Bessler, like a picador, pricked at the protective hide that Nick used to maintain his self-control. Nick explained his feelings and his fears in an interview.

"I look at the clock. It's twenty minutes to two and I am in math and I am comfortable and safe. But in five minutes I have to go to social studies and Mr. B. gets mad at me all the time. I'm nervous about what he will do and I am more nervous about what I will do to him." About six weeks later, Nick lost his temper and made threatening gestures toward Mr. Bessler and was suspended from school for ten days.

Inadequate Instruction. In addition to poverty, dirt, and excessive harshness, failing schools may suffer from teachers who simply didn't know their instructional content. A third-grade teacher told her students, who were sitting on the floor in front of her and paying close attention, that an obstetrician is the doctor who makes eyeglasses, pulling hers off to illustrate the point. The first student in that class who needed corrective lenses may have encountered a surprise.

Sometimes, a teacher confused students even when the students and the teacher were all working from the same textbook. In one class, the subject was social studies and the fifth-graders were preparing for a test.

First, the teacher asked, "How did the settlers come across the Bering Strait?" The student he called on said, "It was dry land," which was the answer in the book right in front of the students. The teacher, who had the teachers' manual right in front of him, said, "No, it was ice." The students did not try to correct or question him.

Later, the teacher put five questions on the board and assigned them as a test. Number 5 asked, "Why do you think that the Bering Strait was once dry land?" How could they possibly answer that? He told them ten minutes ago that it was ice and there was no clue in the book as to why it was dry land. It simply stated the facts. No discussion took place to help the students understand the significance of the Bering Strait and how its terrain changed over time.

Lowest- and Highest-Achieving Students. Failing schools do not do well by students at either end of the learning spectrum. Admittedly, students who somehow reach sixth and seventh grade without learning to read are an immense challenge, especially when they represent the majority of the student body.

At Evergreen Middle School, which served about six hundred sixth- and seventh-graders, a gifted and talented program involved about 20 percent of the students. The teacher who taught this class for two years said that the qualifying students were those who scored as proficient on standardized tests of reading. She said, "The difference was that these students can read. When kids can read, there is no limit on what they can achieve." The implication was that the rest of the sixth- and seventh-grade students could not read.

A middle-school principal, who was new to a school where teachers listed discipline problems as their greatest challenge, brought two lists to a faculty meeting. One was a list of students failing English/language arts. The other was a list of students who had multiple discipline referrals and suspensions. Except for two names, the lists were identical.

She asked the teachers to reflect on the meaning of the two lists. After a few minutes one said, "I suppose that they would rather be known as troublemakers than be ridiculed by their peers because they can't read." It was a true "aha" moment for the teachers, who spent the rest of the meeting looking for solutions for their troublemakers who were also nonreaders.

Intellectually gifted students offer still another challenge to a failing school. Research tells us that they exist in impoverished schools in about the same proportion as in more affluent schools but very few schools in high-poverty areas offer programs for them.

Gifted students need programs that challenge their abilities. In 1987, Senator Edward Kennedy sponsored a bipartisan act called "Star Schools." The program, which focused on math and science, included distance learning for gifted students living in rural areas. The research included observing programs in which gifted students from many schools came together via the Internet and learned advanced physics from an equally gifted teacher.

The researcher watched from the control room as the teacher called her class together, "Greenville, are you there?" and a group of students would appear on her screen, all looking eager. "Royalton, are you there?" and a new group of students filled another screen. The students loved the teacher and they also bonded with each other. One day, they talked about figuring out how to have a "distance prom."

This class changed the lives of the student participants. Glen said, "It's just me and a computer sitting in a broom closet in my school, but I'm finally learning something." Another said that before the program he was the class clown because school bored him so much. The technology has moved on tremendously since that research study was conducted but the principle of challenging the minds of intellectually gifted students remains the same.

Afterschool programs can meet at least some gifted students' needs if the schools would only adopt them. The trend, however, is for afterschool programs to focus on reinforcing academic achievement rather than oriented toward enrichment activities. Frequently, students are put into afterschool programs to make them do their homework. Imagine that you are a student who doesn't love school to begin with, who finishes a long day, and then has to stay in the same building and do another ninety minutes of the same work.

Cognizant of the need to serve these students, a very poor urban district created a program for gifted students in its elementary schools. So many of the students came to school knowing little or no English that it was a challenge to identify those who would benefit from the program.

The program director reported, "We have three ways to choose students for the gifted program. We may see their intelligence in test results, teachers may nominate them, or students can come and knock on my door and say they want to be in the program. The students who knock on the door do just as well as the others."

Tamika was a third-grader in a school that offered nothing to its gifted students. At nine years old, Tamika could finish the average third-grade worksheet before the teacher had handed out sheets to all the other children. She learned that if she told the teacher that she had finished the assignment, she would just get another worksheet. So, she often sat scribbling in a notebook that she kept inside her desk.

It turned out that Tamika was writing a novel. She was a shy little girl and did not want to share the story until it was finished. Even then, she allowed the researcher to read only the ending. "Two years later he was still the same. His mom was sick of fighting with him. He was still in the third grade and he did not care at all."

Blaming the Students. In some schools, no matter what goes wrong, the students get the blame. At the Haviland Elementary School, the third-grade students were excited that Ms. Johnson had promised them a science experiment. With her back to the class, she began slowly writing on the board the list of materials the students would need to do the experiment.

As time went on, the students became bored and restless, the more so when Ms. Johnson sat down at her desk and silently read in the teachers' manual the directions for doing the experiment. Eighteen minutes had elapsed and, except for copying the list of materials, the students had done nothing. Nor did they know what or why they were experimenting.

Not surprisingly, the class got noisy and unruly. Ms. Johnson grew angrier by the minute and threatened the students with cancellation of the experiment. As the teacher berated the class, a student said under her breath, "I don't care, I don't care, I don't care."

Staring hopefully at the board, another student asked, "Are we building an explosive device?" But no experiment took place since Ms. Johnson decided that the class was "too naughty" to deserve one. "That's what happens when

I try to do something nice for you," she said as she erased the list of materials from the board.

CHARTER SCHOOLS: A FAULTY SOLUTION

The intractability of failing schools on the one hand and the desire to provide better options for the students who attended those schools on the other hand, became catalysts for the development of charter schools. Although they differ in many ways from state to state, charter schools generally share the following characteristics:

- They can choose their own curriculum.
- They have control over their own budgets.
- They can hire and fire teachers.
- Teachers are free from union rules.

In exchange for those freedoms, the charter schools are responsible for demonstrating academic success within the five-year period of their charter. If they don't succeed, the schools may lose their charters. Over time, some charter schools have become more like the schools they replaced, failures and all.

Charter Schools in Massachusetts. The history of the charter school movement in Massachusetts is an instructive story of charter schools that lost the qualities that originally made them different from other public schools.

In 1993, the governor's office, rather than the state education agency, issued the original school charters. Each charter school reported only to the governor. The schools were geographically dispersed around the state. Some were operated by for-profit organizations, but most were nonprofits organized around instructional themes and well-known structured curricula. One school, for example, was organized around the seven golden virtues: courage, moderation, justice, responsibility, prudence, friendship, and wonder. A fifth-grade student said, "It's hard to talk to my friends from other schools. They don't even know what the virtues are."

The schools proved so popular in urban areas that students were chosen by lottery from among the applicants, while their families stood watching, some praying for their children's acceptance. One woman fell to her knees praising Jesus when her son's name was called.

The teachers in the first set of charter schools were those who had always envisioned giving more to their students; many of them said they were frustrated by the union rules, particularly the constraints on the number of hours they could spend in school.

Now able to work hours and hours before and after school, the teachers drove themselves to exhaustion. Several teachers cried during their interviews, saying, "The students need so much. I'm working three times harder than I ever did before and I still am not getting the results I thought I would."

These original charter schools had to find space where they could. One middle school occupied a storefront in a strip mall next door to a barber shop. The students told stories of people coming into the school looking for haircuts. One suggested, "We ought to have a course in barbering so we can help those guys." In that high-energy, creative environment, it almost sounded like a reasonable idea.

In addition to serving as alternatives for students, Massachusetts presented the charter schools as laboratories of educational innovation, which would then be disseminated to other public schools. In 1996, a research study was commissioned to see how well the ideas of these laboratories of innovation were working.

The charter schools were humming with energy and new ideas. The schools had made changes in the amount of learning time and academic support available to students, as well as providing individualized curriculum and encouraging family involvement in the instructional process.

While the charter schools appeared to have innovative ideas to share, the schools that had lost students to the charter schools were having none of it. First, several principals insisted that charter schools were not real public schools. Then they resorted to another myth about charter schools, namely that they are so different from "regular" schools that nothing can be learned from them. One teacher said bluntly, "Over my dead body, I'll copy anything from over there. Anyway, the kids will be back as soon as the novelty wears off."

One elementary-school principal who had lost many students to a charter school said, "I'm glad those kids are gone; in one fell swoop, I got rid of all my most difficult parents."

Who were the most difficult parents? Apparently, they were those who challenged the status quo, those who tried to intervene in the system, and those who wanted a better education for their children. Without those trouble-making parents, the school was free to remain static, holding on to students whose families did not understand the significance of this opportunity for their children.

Meanwhile, the state education agency was aghast at having schools operating outside of their purview and lobbied successfully to bring the charter schools under their umbrella. Several histories of charter schools in Massachusetts do not even mention the time they spent reporting directly to the governor.

Horace Mann Schools. The Massachusetts legislature created Horace Mann schools in 1997. While Commonwealth Charter schools are accountable to the state, Horace Mann schools belong to the school district that created and governs them. In fact, to obtain their "charter," the plan for a Horace Mann school must be approved by the local school committee, the superintendent of schools, and the president of the teachers' union. In other words, they adhere closely to the same rules as the schools they supposedly replaced.

THE ROLE OF FREE ENTERPRISE IN EDUCATION

For proponents of charter schools, freedom of choice is a logical extension of competition in the marketplace. At the heart of this competition is money. Students carry with them the state per pupil expenditure (PPE), the amount allocated by the state for their education. The amount of funding varies by state from about $7,000 per pupil to almost $23,000.

When students vacate their seat in one school and enroll in a charter school, they take their PPE with them. The more students who opt for charter schools, the less funding other public schools have to spend on teachers' salaries and benefits, and the purchase of resources. It's a downward spiral for those schools.

A focus group of high-school teachers expressed their feelings about the success of two charter schools in a neighboring district. "Sometimes the charter school drains off some of the kids you'd like to keep. Of course, they have the cream of the crop."

"The teachers in the neighboring district have worked so hard for so many years. To put upon them the burden of a charter school isn't fair. I feel for them. It's free enterprise and people are going wherever they want to go. When you have lower economic areas they're almost driven to send their child to a charter school."

The hypothesis that charter schools would serve as laboratories of innovation posited that regular public schools would then pick up on the innovations and through this process would improve schools. This hypothesis has not proved true in Massachusetts and, in fact, the prevailing attitude on the part of regular public schools remains one of hostility.

But what are students doing as commodities in the marketplace anyway? Are they not all entitled to the best possible education we can provide? What happens to the students whose families do not have the interest, knowledge, or energy to go through the charter school application process? Are they to be left to languish in schools that are falling further and further behind?

The road to school improvement needs to lead straight to the schools that need the most help, not to byways and detours like charter schools. The natural bottom line of charter school success is that failing schools are systematically ignored and left to die. This will happen because of the inertia of policy makers and an implicit assumption that the leftover students are disposable and are not worthy of innovation and excellence.

IN YOUR TOOLBOX

A copy of the evaluation tool that supports this chapter, *Make Your School a Welcoming Place* appears in the appendix. It is also available for free download per request to nbrighamassoc@yahoo.com.

Chapter 11

How Useful Are External Interventions?

So often, interventions to improve the skills of teachers and the performance of students turn out to be like spoons that are too short. They stir and stir, but never reach the bottom of the bowl where the schools with the greatest needs are left to flounder on their own.

Schools that are on the bottom because they consistently underperform academically also tend to be disorganized, demoralized, and mismanaged. They keep posting failing scores year after year, despite changes in faculty and leadership.

Desperate to bring about improvement, some administrators are driven to seek help from outside providers. As one frustrated administrator said reluctantly, "I guess it's time to bring in the consultants."

At this point, the administrators have a choice between two approaches. One is to buy a packaged program intervention to address the needs of all the failing schools. The other is to embark on a customized approach in which consultants are assigned to individual schools to address their unique problems.

PACKAGED PROGRAM INTERVENTIONS

The education establishment makes huge investments in programs created by outside developers that promise to improve reading, math, science, instructional skills, or behavior. The program developers are experts in their fields and have conducted extensive research to support the premises of their programs. Often, the programs can point to credible outside evaluations to prove that they have demonstrated success in other school districts.

The developers also act as vendors for their programs, which may cost $800 to $1,000 per pupil. What are the program developers selling? Almost always, there is the cost of professional development for teachers and an investment in new materials and curricula. The cost may also include sending administrators and classroom teachers to regional or national conferences. The package may also offer periodic visits by the program developers or their surrogates to give feedback on how well the schools are implementing the new program.

As part of the adoption process, the developers give program introduction sessions, including presentations, videos, testimonials, and the opportunity to examine the program materials. At the end of this presentation, teachers in the audience vote on whether they want to "buy into" the new program. A high level of buy in by teachers is vigorously touted in final negotiations with the school district, but it can be misleading.

For example, the developer says, "98 percent of the faculty at Spruce Elementary School buy into our program." When you interview the teachers at Spruce, you learn there is more to the story. "I would have voted for any-thing that brought more resources to the school." "We have no place to go but up." "It's got to be better than what we have now." It turns out that they are voting less *for* the program than *against* the status quo, and this is most true of teachers in the poorest, lowest-performing schools in a district.

Initial seed money for programs may come from a charitable foundation or, more likely, the federal government. Seed money usually supports the program for three years, at which point the local district is expected to pick up the tab for the program and sustain it with local resources.

The three-year lifespan of outside funding is arbitrary. It assumes one year of startup and training, one year of full implementation, and a third year of institutionalization. Then, the new program is supposed to become an integral part of the school and district. The expectation that a district will sustain the program rests on some shaky assumptions.

The first, and most costly, assumption is that the teachers who have been extensively trained at a high cost will remain at the school to implement the program over the course of several years. Since failing schools have high teacher turnover rates, this is unlikely to happen. Many programs wither over time because they do not have plans in place to train teachers who are new to the school program. Ideally, the new teachers would get the same training as that given to the original teacher cadre, but it seldom happens that way.

The district, which is no longer receiving funded services, is left to find time to bring groups of new teachers together, obtain the services of a trainer, and provide substitute teachers to take over classrooms while the new teachers are being trained. In lieu of training, a mentor teacher who is already trained is given the sole responsibility for orienting new teachers to the program.

The second assumption is that the state or school district has the funds available to pick up the costs of continuing the program at the end of three years. In the current era of reduced school funding, that option has become more and more unlikely.

Especially costly are the salaries for new positions that were funded by the program. Often teachers who have been relieved of classroom duties serve as coordinators. These teachers were trained more thoroughly than others and served as program coordinators or as mentors to teachers struggling to implement the program. When the funding ends, so do those positions and these teachers go back to their classrooms.

The third assumption is that the program will not encounter competition during the institutionalization process. This assumption ignores the likelihood that competing program opportunities will come along to push the old program aside.

The competing program will bring in more outside funding, additional professional development, new materials, and other resources. Administrators cannot be blamed for wanting to take advantage of funding opportunities even if the next program ignores or contradicts the premises of the old one.

New posters go up on the walls and the old ones are rolled up and put in storage rooms. "Last year," a teacher said, "we were a school excited about reading, but this year, we're all about being critical friends."

MAKING IT AT FONTAINE ELEMENTARY SCHOOL

Making It is a schoolwide reading program for all students in grades 1 through 3, which is designed to serve low-income schools that struggle with teaching reading in the early grades. The promise of *Making It* is that, if the program is implemented with fidelity, all students will read on grade level by the end of third grade.

To meet its objectives, *Making It*, which is a highly scripted program, must be implemented not just with fidelity but with precision. For ninety minutes every day, students are grouped with others on the same reading level, no matter what grade they are in. In a school implementing *Making It*, all the teachers are teaching reading at the same time for ninety minutes every morning. This program requirement means that students move from one classroom to another twice a day, so they can be instructed with others reading on the same level.

Making It was one of the programs evaluated as part of a federal assessment of evidence-based approaches to teaching reading in disadvantaged elementary schools. One of the schools participating was Fontaine Elementary School.

The poverty level at Fontaine was demonstrated every day by the "Three Sheets" rule. At bathroom break time, the teacher stood in the doorway of the classroom and handed each student exactly three sheets of toilet paper from a roll she held in her hand. A parent reported that her daughter often needed more but was embarrassed to ask. So, her mother tucked extra toilet paper into all the daughter's pockets before she left for school.

One hundred percent of the students were receiving free or reduced lunch. With the exception of four or five students, all the students were ethnic minorities and, since it was a neighborhood school, they almost all lived in the surrounding federally funded, low-income housing project.

At Fontaine, pandemonium reigned in the halls as students left their own classrooms and went to other classrooms to spend ninety minutes of *Making It* with students reading on the same level. The researchers were assigned to Shadow students who had been placed in different groups. Moses, although he was in third grade, went to a low second-grade reading group.

Kendira, however, stayed in her own classroom while other students in the high-achieving first-grade reading group came in and tried to find space for their materials among the debris left on their desks by the departing students. Because teachers remained in their classrooms to receive the incoming students, no adult was stationed in the hall to prevent dawdling, bickering, and fighting, all of which occurred daily.

The transition was supposed to take five minutes; most days it took ten. Added to that was the time it took to settle the incoming students, deal with behavior issues, take attendance, and hand out materials. The ninety minutes might, on a bad day, shrink to seventy-five.

The activities that took place during those seventy-five to ninety minutes were also highly scripted. They incorporated phonics, decoding, and other research-based approaches to learning to read. In the first-grade classroom at Fontaine, the observer seldom saw the sequence happen as prescribed. The teacher would become absorbed in one activity and let the next one slide, or more frequently, classroom-management problems took time away from instruction.

A key element of the program was to regroup the students every eight weeks according to their progress in learning to read. Based on the assessment, a student might be moved to a new group either more or less advanced than the previous one. If Moses, for example, had a reading breakthrough, he might be moved from his low second-grade group to a high second-grade group where he could build on his progress.

Unfortunately, the school program coordinator at Fontaine, who was trained to test and regroup students, was out sick for several weeks in the middle of the year. Since he was the only person trained to perform this task, no regrouping was done during the entire year. Whatever group you were in at the end of September was where you were in June.

Making It was an appropriate program for improving reading at Fontaine, but it was not implemented completely or correctly. Fontaine simply did not have the leadership skills, the management skills, or the determination to make this or any program successful. Schools that cannot manage themselves are unlikely to be able to manage even the most appropriate interventions to improve them.

Fontaine needed help that was so extensive and so expensive that it was beyond the resources of the district to address all its needs. A few years later, Fontaine was closed and the students were assigned to other schools.

SESAME READING AT COLONIST MIDDLE SCHOOL

The *Sesame Reading* program is another intervention focused on students reading below grade level. The program pulls students from their regular reading classes to be instructed by teachers who have been trained to follow an exacting script. *Sesame Reading* instruction combines whole-class, small-group, and individual instruction via software that tracks their progress.

Sesame Reading was implemented at Colonist Middle School, a stately, elegant old school building, imposing from the outside but crowded, shabby, and often chaotic on the inside. In the previous five years, the school has had four principals. The student population was almost completely comprised of ethnic minorities, and 98 percent of the students received free or reduced lunch, the most common marker of student poverty.

Into this context, the district introduced *Sesame Reading*. At Colonist Middle School, *Sesame Reading* was a triage program aimed at those students who were presumed to need just a few months of intensive attention to reach grade level in reading. So many of the elements of *Sesame Reading* were distorted in the implementation process that the program had little resemblance to the original model.

For one thing, the program is designed for a maximum class size of fifteen students per teacher for a ninety-minute period. Colonist Middle School crammed twenty-six students into each class period and cut the time to forty-five minutes. Since the teachers never analyzed the reading scores of the students to see if they were ready to exit the program, the same students just stayed in it year after year and other students never got the opportunity to enroll.

A teacher said, "Is *Sesame Reading* doing it? I haven't seen any proof one way or the other and for some of the kids this is their third year in it. Where is the proof that the program works? Where is the progress? Some kids are going to get their postgraduate degree in it."

Since *Sesame Reading* was a pullout program, the general English/reading classroom teachers were left with classes consisting of the best readers and the worst readers, and they had a difficult time finding ways of differentiating instruction to bridge the gap. One teacher took six weeks of stress-related illness leave as a result of her frustration and then retired at the end of the year.

It was the district's decision to purchase *Sesame Reading* and then to let the schools do with it what they would. Colonist Middle School implemented a program that addressed a small segment of students with reading issues and ignored the majority of students with greater needs.

They chose a triage approach when much more substantial help was needed. The students in the program were one to two years below grade level while the nonreaders, who had somehow reached middle school with virtually no skills, were not touched by the program. *Sesame Reading* was not the program Colonist Middle School needed and then, of course, it was implemented so badly that just a few students ever benefitted.

PROGRAMS OF CUSTOMIZED SUPPORT

In their quest to improve school performance, administrators may bring in consultants with specific expertise they believe the schools need most. Based on failing test scores in writing, for example, a writing coach might work in several schools in a district over the course of a week.

The consultant meets with different groups of teachers to introduce new strategies to teach writing. For schools with multiple needs, the district may hire several consultants who come in and out during the week.

Showing the visitors' book, a school secretary complained, "I feel like I'm running a hotel here. In and out, in and out." The book showed that five different consultants had signed in during a single day, all pursuing different objectives, from writing to classroom management. According to custom, each of the consultants had a teacher liaison, who was responsible for rounding up the participating teachers, providing coverage for their classes, and finding a private space to accommodate the group.

Schools with the greatest needs are the most likely to have trouble managing logistics. It is not unusual to find consultants without a space to work and they may not have access to the teachers they have come to help. One literacy coach was scheduled to meet with twenty-three teachers during a six-period school day. Nine actually showed up and not one of the teachers scheduled for an afterschool workshop attended.

Why? Teachers in some schools apparently believe that when the district brings in outside expertise, it is somehow denigrating the skills of their own faculty. For example, "She comes in once a month with a focus on writing. She's been great, but I like the idea of our own teachers doing it. I would like to see the facilitator working along with them."

Another teacher said, "What I use in the classroom is an amalgam of things, but I think we learn best from our colleagues who have something to offer. Our own faculty knows as much about literacy as anybody in the district. We don't rely enough on our own gifts and talents within the building. Fellow teachers are the best! They know our weaknesses, know our clientele."

SCHOOL COACHES IN DALTON CITY

The cadre of instructional coaches who served the failing schools in Dalton City were experts in instruction, who pursued a highly individualized approach to every school. They met once a month with their project director to discuss their progress, challenges, and suggestions for improvement. In theory, the approach was optimal for meeting the needs of the school, but in practice it was subject to immense constraints.

Under the provisions of No Child Left Behind (NCLB) schools that failed to make "adequate yearly progress" for three consecutive years became subject to corrective action. In Dalton City, six middle schools and two high schools were in that category when the state department of education assumed responsibility for the district. The state officials, who had never borne this obligation before, struggled with how to balance support for local improvement efforts while simultaneously holding the district accountable for making academic progress.

Their eventual decision was to place highly skilled instructional coaches into each of the failing schools to provide customized, intensive, ongoing support to the principal and teachers. The state department of education signed a contract with a consulting company known for its expertise in providing technical assistance. The company assigned one coach to each school and asked them to find their own way to approach the task, based on the needs and receptivity of the schools.

Even the top school officers in the state were not quite sure how well the coaching was going to work. One said, "I created a model and threw them in. The expectation of their role is if they build good relationships and strengthen the infrastructure within the schools, good things will happen."

When hiring the consultants, one thing the state did not do, and probably should have done, was to discuss putting the coaches in the schools with administrators at the district level, especially the newly hired superintendent.

District administrators did not forgive this omission and for two years, the coaches were invisible to the leaders of the district.

Their work was not rewarded; in fact, their very names were not recognized as it was apparently district policy to ignore them. Since the coaches reported directly to the state department of education and not to the district they became, as in some ancient fiefdom, nonpersons to the superintendent's staff. The superintendent himself was actively hostile to the work of the coaches and, whether intentionally or not, threw a series of stumbling blocks into their path.

The first year the coaches started operating, their very broad mission was to help the principal and teachers, raise morale, and improve instruction. They did so in a variety of ways. Some found great success while others encountered uphill battles.

Mentoring the Principal. One facilitator, who was himself a former principal, worked closely with a new and inexperienced principal. He functioned as an assistant principal and instructional leader of the school. He went into classrooms, observed, and advised teachers. He had complete access to the principal and all the teachers.

The coach hand-scheduled all incoming students for placement in the reading program. For the second year, he hoped to work on issues of discipline and civility. However, the principal was reassigned and the new principal severely curtailed his role.

This coach was one of several who worked directly with principals, mentoring them on the important components of effective leadership such as presiding at meetings, dealing with parents, and observing teachers and providing them with helpful feedback. Then, during the summer, the superintendent fired one principal and reassigned all but one of the others, shuffling them from one failing school to another. He called this "holding them accountable."

This wholesale reassignment of principals was a huge blow to the coaches. They had now spent a year helping a principal to become a leader for school A and now faced starting all over again with principal B who didn't know the teachers, the students, or the history of school A. The state did nothing about it, primarily because they didn't know about it until it was done.

Working with School Improvement Teams. During the first year, other coaches worked with the School Improvement Teams (SITs) which were generally made up of veteran teachers who were the real leaders of the schools. These veteran teachers had seen principals, superintendents, and programs come and go and they were cynical about the system.

The district had tasked each school to create a customized improvement plan and promised that if the schools wrote good plans, they would be implemented the following year. On that basis, coaches managed to convince the teachers to become actively engaged in writing a new school-improvement plan, "To create the school you want to see."

With advice from the coach, the lowest of the middle schools in terms of academic achievement managed to write a customized plan including major changes in curriculum, scheduling, and assessment. At the end of the year, the principal showed them the comments their work had received from the district.

Among other things, the plan was deemed "thoughtful" and a "blueprint" for the school's future. The teachers beamed at the praise because they didn't often get positive feedback from the district or anyone else.

This school's new principal said he had only the newly completed plan to guide him when he started at the school the following July. He said he intended to carry it out to the letter, but was forestalled by the district, which informed him that he would be given a new plan. He said, "We're waiting for the district to come up with new plans. As I understand it, the district does that now."

For some unknown reason, the superintendent had decided that the plans created by the schools were not strong enough to get the approval of the state. Whether the state said or even intimated that was never clear, but the superintendent decided to "pre-populate" all the school plans: that is to rewrite the most important and most customized portions, such as curriculum and scheduling. Unlike the original plans, the pre-populated plans were all exactly alike. The schools had handed in plans tailored to fit their schools' needs; now, apparently, one size fits all.

Using Data to Plan Instruction. Another area to which the coaches brought their expertise was helping teachers to use data to plan instruction. Dalton City was fortunate to have midterm assessments administered in the middle of the school year, so teachers didn't have to wait until the end of the year to see where their students were failing.

Meeting with teachers in each department, the coaches helped them to interpret and use the data from the midterm assessments to improve instruction and to help the teachers become more diagnostic and reflective. They brought in new instructional strategies, visited classrooms, and provided feedback. Sometimes, a coach would take over a class and model a new instructional strategy.

In another surprise move, the superintendent decided to suspend the use of the midterm assessments for at least a year. He questioned the extent to which the assessments were research-based and made no commitment either to replace or revise them. This left the coaches with one less tool for improving instruction in classrooms.

A Circumscribed Role. Not all the coaches were able to find an entry point with either the principal or the majority of teachers. One coach decided to focus almost entirely on working with a small group of teachers who volunteered to participate in a book group, based on a book containing strategies for teaching writing.

The group met after school and the members were compensated for their time through a small grant. The participants agreed to do the homework, apply the strategies in their classrooms, and have the facilitator observe their instruction and provide feedback. When the principal found out how well received the workshop was, he asked the coach to work with a larger group of teachers on classroom-management skills.

The coaching model that the state set up for the Dalton City schools was an excellent fit to the schools' needs. The state's willingness to allow a flexible approach and the expertise of the coaches convinced the teachers and principals in most of the schools to accept and appreciate help.

However, no program is immune to sabotage either from within or without. The superintendent's high-handed interference threatened to undo the work of the coaches throughout their time in Dalton City, but the state was ultimately responsible. Having launched them into the maelstrom, the state officials left them unprotected.

In the end, the problems lie not with the particular interventions, whether they are packaged or customized, but with the assumptions made about the implementation and the results of the interventions. It starts at the top. Administrators invest in one-size-fits-all program and assume that schools will implement them with fidelity. Sadly, the schools that need help the most are likely to mismanage the implementation process and fail to achieve the program goals.

Administrators also seem to believe that schools with multiple needs require multiple consultants. Again, the neediest schools find it difficult to manage the logistics of the consultant visits and fail to benefit as they should. Perhaps the greatest assumption of the experts in education is that they can drop assistance indiscriminately on schools and achieve positive outcomes. They are wrong.

Section Four

TESTING AND EVALUATION

Chapter 12

The National Obsession with Testing Students

The proliferation of standardized state student-achievement tests produced legions of passionate advocates and opponents, but its most unfortunate consequence was that it exposed the unwillingness of many educators to take any responsibility for students' failure. Time that might have been spent improving instruction was instead spent undermining the testing process by dumbing down the tests, tampering with the scoring, or by blaming students and their families for failure.

For many years, measuring student achievement was an adjunct to instruction, an important component of the education process, but not the primary one. With the advent of NCLB, the George W. Bush national education initiative, standardized student achievement tests soon became an obsession, and instruction threatened to become an adjunct to testing.

The federal NCLB legislation required states to set standards for student achievement and then create assessments to measure whether students were reaching the standards. The federal role in NCLB sounded more powerful than it actually was because the power to set the standards and create the tests was left to the states.

The NCLB designers believed that testing based on standards would be a vehicle for improving instruction. In one scenario, teachers would hold meetings by grade level to review the state achievement-test results item by item, looking for important concepts that many students failed to grasp. Then they would devise more effective ways of reteaching that concept.

In some schools this scenario played out successfully, but in many others, the test results didn't reach the teachers until the tested students had moved on to the next grade. In some schools, teachers had no structured time during the day to meet as a group, or there were no appropriate professional-development resources available to them.

As the tests multiplied from grade to grade and subject to subject, so did the fervor of the testing advocates and opponents. The advocates maintained it was only reasonable to find out what students knew after completing a year of instruction. The opponents insisted that students were being overtested. One teacher said, "The roast will never get cooked if you keep opening the oven to check on it."

Faced with the reality of implementing NCLB, some education officials began to have nightmares. They imagined newspaper headlines that proclaimed, "New tests show massive failures" or, "It turns out Johnny *can't* read." Hastily putting on their thinking caps, these officials came up with three solutions: (1) simplify the content of the tests; (2) alter the scoring of the tests to produce positive results; or (3) find someone else to blame for failure.

Simplifying the Tests

Some state education departments simply dumbed down the standards and the tests so that students were not challenged to meet true grade-level expectations. For example, let's say you were a fourth-grader in State A taking a test that included a question to determine how well you understand the difference between fact and opinion.

The State A test asks:

Which sentence tells a fact, not an opinion?

1. Cats are better than dogs.
2. Cats climb trees better than dogs.
3. Cats are prettier than dogs.
4. Cats have nicer fur than dogs.

Now, let's say you moved to State B and were tested on the same skill. In State B, the test item for the same grade level was *How Much Land Does a Man Need?* (Tolstoy).

"So Pahom was well contented, and everything would have been right if the neighboring peasants would only not have trespassed on his wheat fields and meadows. He appealed to them most civilly, but they still went on: now the herdsmen would let the village cows stray into his meadows, then horses from the night pasture would get among his corn.

"Pahom turned them out again and again, and forgave their owners, and for a long time he forbore to prosecute anyone. But at last he lost patience and complained to the District Court."

What is a fact from this passage?

1. Pahom owns a vast amount of land.
2. The peasants' intentions are evil.
3. Pahom is a wealthy man.
4. Pahom complained to the District Court.

This example illustrates not only the immense difference in tests among states, but suggests the dangerous long-term effects of shortchanging students' learning. Few skills are more important to citizens in a democracy than being able to tell the difference between a fact and an opinion.

Watch the news any night and you are bombarded with opinions stated as facts. To become informed voters, students need to understand the fact/opinion concept in all its complexity. It needs to be taught more deeply, more effectively, more often, and at many different grade levels.

TAMPERING WITH THE SCORING RUBRIC

The range of student outcomes on standardized achievement tests is a continuum from *Not Proficient* at one end to *Advanced* at the other. There are cutoff points for each category and the goal is to have as many students as possible in the top two: *Proficient* and *Advanced*.

Some state education agencies yielded to the temptation to alter the categories of proficiency. By simply moving the cutoff point between "not proficient" and "proficient," these officials could change students' scores from failure to success. With one stroke of the pen, students were officially reading on grade level, no matter what their actual performance was.

Fortunately, there was a gotcha test to expose this particular piece of trickery. The National Assessment of Education Progress (NAEP), administered to a sample of fourth- and eighth-graders in every state, demonstrated where chicanery was taking place. The NAEP assesses the same skills and abilities as state standardized tests, but the results may be very different.

For example, in one state the published state standardized achievement test results showed that 89 percent of fourth-grade students were scoring in the proficient range, while on the NAEP, only 26 percent of students in the state scored in that range, a difference of 63 percent.

What a terrible disservice to students! The first three grades are the "learning to read" grades; beginning in fourth grade, students are "reading to learn," that is, expected to understand written materials at grade level. A student who does not know how to read at the end of third grade is slowly beginning to circle the drain of educational failure and no amount of game playing at the state level will change that.

Triage in the Classroom

Various instructional strategies were implemented by schools in order to raise test scores. One was determining which students came closest to meeting the proficiency standard and then engaging in "triage."

The chosen students would get extra practice and attention in the classroom, an additional reading period, for example. The hope was that with just one extra push, these students would move up a notch on the test and consequently the whole school would look better.

A classroom teacher might work in the front of the room with the potentially proficient students, while others, who needed more than just a push to get over the top, struggled with seat work or, worst-case scenario, spent their time coloring. Triage is a valuable tool in the medical profession, but it's hard to condone in education. You might as well announce publicly that the school has just given up on its neediest students.

BLAMING THE VICTIMS

Some states opted to punish students who repeatedly did poorly on their standardized tests. The punishments were sometimes severe. For example, in one state, the policy was that students who failed the state standardized test three times would be sent to an alternative school rather than the high school their friends attended.

A middle school, where many students were at risk of failure, convened a group of teachers across content areas to find ways to improve the achievement of specific at-risk students. The teachers went name by name through the list of ninth-grade students and discussed each one in turn.

"He could do the work, but he's never here. He's absent because his girlfriend is having a baby and he's working to pay for it." Another teacher added, "Ah, that's why he's so sleepy all the time."

"She's sick all the time, sickle cell anemia. Her mama ran out of medicine, can't afford it. When she's on the medicine, she's so sleepy she can't stay awake in school." "She has to stay home with her baby. It's too bad. Her grades are excellent." "She's pregnant. Only seventy to eighty pounds and she really needs prenatal vitamins. She's either dragging around or out of school."

Not one further word was said about addressing the horrific problems the group had put on the table. The meeting ended with a lively discussion about which students would get to attend the ninth-grade prom. The teachers agreed to use the threat of not going to the prom to put pressure on the students to "keep their shirt tails tucked in," that is, obey the dress code for the five days until the prom. One teacher said she told the girls, "Don't take the tags off that prom dress."

A more common form of blaming the victims came to the fore when some classroom teachers convinced themselves that students didn't learn the material taught to them because they didn't want to, and their parents didn't care. In one focus group, seven bitter veteran teachers joined in heartily to blame the victims. "They are apathetic, disobedient, disrespectful. When you ask them to do any work they act like you are telling them to go play in traffic!"

Another teacher added, "They come from a culture where failure is accepted. It's demographics. These students just have no drive. There is a cultural acceptance of failure here, as in 'Hey, I got a D, High five!' That's a celebration of failure."

Teachers like this also insist that students don't care about their achievement test scores. "They just bubble in the circles and get on with their lives." One teacher even maintained that the students gave wrong answers just to punish their teachers. "They know we are judged in part by our students' test scores, so they put down wrong answers to get their revenge."

One teacher in the group stated that she refused to post a scoring rubric in her classroom even though the school had adopted rubrics in order to objectify the grading process. Rubrics delineate the criteria for assigning *acceptable*, *good*, or *excellent* grades.

The rationale is that a rubric posted in the classroom allows teachers and students alike to understand what an excellent paper looks like versus one that is just acceptable. This teacher's explanation for refusing to post the rubric was that her sixth graders would use it to see how little they could do and still pass, and that's all the effort they would make.

Another avenue for shifting blame to the students and their families is to invoke "student apathy," a popular term used by teachers and administrators to explain students' failure. A frequently cited cause of apathy is that families don't make their children go to bed early enough and the students come to school sleepy every day.

That may be true, but sleepiness and apathy are not the same thing. Sleepiness can be addressed by taking the students out in the fresh air or by keeping them active in the classroom, or even by letting them put their heads down on their desks for a few minutes. Some teachers will find out why a student is always sleepy and respond sensitively.

For example, the observer saw a boy sleeping soundly at the table in the small, dark, in-school suspension room. The principal said, "That's Evan. His parents have abandoned the family and now his twenty-one-year-old sister is in charge of the other children. She has loud parties almost every night and

Evan's bed is the living room sofa. The poor kid never gets any sleep so the teachers take turns sending him down here for a nap."

Apathy is something else entirely. It is defined as a lack of feelings or reaction to things that are generally considered interesting. Teachers who are quick to see the students as apathetic are less likely to realize that their classes are not interesting.

Slavish adherence to the textbook, the use of multiple worksheets, not allowing students to discuss their work or move around the classroom, are all root causes of apathy. And in some classes, those things happen day after day after day.

WRITING ACROSS THE CURRICULUM

The writing portion of the standardized achievement tests gives students the most trouble. Here, rather than filling in the circle next to a multiple-choice question, the student must write an essay on some prescribed topic. Schools try all kinds of stratagems to improve students' writing skills. One is called "writing across the curriculum."

"Every teacher in our school is a writing teacher," a principal declared proudly, but actually that is not possible, since teaching writing is a skill and a specific set of practices. You can no more label the whole faculty writing teachers than you can label them nurses or neurosurgeons.

To realize that this approach is a mistake, you need only see a group of students writing about sportsmanship in physical education class, their shoulders hunched as they pore over papers on the gym floor. The gym teacher, his whistle hanging forlornly around his neck, is not a writing teacher and he realizes it even if the principal does not.

Another Unintended Consequence of NCLB

Schools went all out to improve students' test scores, focusing on reading and math in elementary schools because those were originally the only subjects tested. The push to teach to the test relegated some important subjects into minor roles in the curriculum or caused them to vanish entirely.

A superintendent stated, "It is sad, but in this district if it's not tested it's pretty much not taught." The most damaging casualty of the not-tested, not-taught doctrine was civics. Very few states have achievement tests in civics and the subject has generally been relegated to a single unit in American History or offered as an elective course for high-school students.

Students can graduate from high school with no instruction in how and why the government of the United States maintains separation of powers or that the Constitution is the bedrock of our republic. A history teacher told me that most of her graduating seniors did not know the difference between the Declaration of Independence and the Constitution nor why either one was important to their lives.

THE PROBLEMATIC CONCEPT OF "NO FAULT"

It is difficult to believe that some education officials protect their own reputations at the expense of students' success, that a few teachers care more about the dress code then the tragedies of their students' lives, or that educators would blame their own failures on students or their families. But the Blame Game has always flourished in education; it was just exacerbated by the passage of NCLB.

The James Comer School Development Program is a unique approach to education reform in that it focuses on the whole child and the family, as well as on changing attitudes and practices within schools. A Comer school is open and welcoming to the community. You may see parents working as classroom aides or just visiting the school, perhaps to have lunch with their child.

Dr. James Comer was a child psychiatrist rather than an educator and his vision of the Comer program is to "create a just and fair society in which all children have the educational and personal opportunities that will allow them to become successful and satisfied participants in family and civic life."[1]

One precept of the program is "no fault." In a Comer school, teachers are not allowed to blame the students, their families, the teachers in previous grades, or anyone else for where their students are in terms of achievement. In school after school, it turned out that "no fault" was the most difficult part of the Comer program for teachers to implement.

At a faculty meeting, one teacher said flippantly, "No fault is no fun" and another added somberly, "It makes you feel as if you, the teacher, have to take total responsibility for each student in your class." Had Dr. Comer been at the meeting, he would have said that the teacher was exactly right.

The education pendulum appears to be swinging back from the extremes in testing. That might be a good thing except that the education pendulum never seems to stop in the middle, so it is hard to say how far the pendulum will move away from testing or what the consequences will be for students.

NOTE

1. J. P. Comer, *Leave No Child Behind: Preparing Today's Youth for Tomorrow's World* (New Haven, CT: Yale University Press, 2004).

Chapter 13

Do-It-Yourself Evaluations

People tend to see evaluation as an arcane and mysterious art. It is not. While professional evaluators bring specialized experience and expertise to the process, the cost of an outside evaluation can be prohibitive for many programs. In such circumstances, it is a realistic option for program managers to create a credible evaluation on their own.

There is also another option in which the program manager contracts with an evaluator for assistance at key points in the process, such as creating the framework of the evaluation plan, helping to analyze the data, or outline the final report. This is far less costly than a complete outside evaluation, but it leaves a lot of work for the program administrators and staff.

FORMATIVE AND SUMMATIVE EVALUATION

There are two broad categories of evaluation: formative and summative. Formative evaluation is the process of collecting information that will help program managers to make informed decisions about program improvement. Ideally, data collection for formative evaluation purposes is an ongoing component of program development and implementation.

The purpose of summative evaluation is accountability to the stakeholders who have invested in the program. They need to know whether the program was successful and, if so, what was it that made the program work so well. If some components were less successful, they want to know that too. In broadest terms, stakeholders require evidence that clients benefitted from the program and that the outcomes reflect the program's goals.

THE FOUR STEPS IN THE EVALUATION PROCESS

Whether the purpose of the evaluation is formative or summative, it involves four steps that occur in roughly sequential order: planning; collecting information; analyzing and reporting data; and reflecting on the meaning of the information. A program example helps to illustrate how the process works in real life. A running example appears in italics throughout the chapter.

The example highlights a local organization called Audio Materials for the Blind (AMB), a group historically focused on providing audio books and other resources for low-vision adults. With a federal grant, they piloted a program to put audio books into classrooms in order to assist at-risk students with print disabilities. The program also included training the teachers in these classrooms about when and how to use the audio books.

AMB had not included the cost of an outside evaluation in their grant application and consequently very little funding was available for an evaluation. AMB contracted with an evaluator to help develop their overall approach to the evaluation, assist in data analysis, and draft the final report. The remainder of the work, including data collection, was the responsibility of the program staff.

No matter what your purpose in conducting an evaluation, creating a foundation of understanding and establishing buy-ins are the first things you want to accomplish. Begin by convening the program stakeholders, administrators, staff, volunteers, and board members in an initial meeting for resources that are available for the evaluation. The following questions need to be addressed before you proceed with planning an evaluation:

- Who will lead and manage the evaluation?
- What resources in terms of staff time are available to conduct the evaluation and how can they be mobilized?
- What is a realistic time frame for the self-evaluation?

Step One: Planning. After you have decided whether your evaluation is formative or summative, the first task is to clarify the focus of the endeavor. It's not possible to evaluate every facet of every activity, so you want to focus on the activities that address your program goals. You may have more than one focus, but each must be explicitly stated from the beginning.

If the evaluation focuses on implementation, that is formative evaluation, and the information you collect addresses two questions. What are the major activities of the program, and how can they be improved? What factors seem to facilitate or hamper the success of the activities?

If the focus is on program outcomes, that is, summative evaluation, you need to review the goals of the program in order to develop evaluation questions that will show to what extent the outcomes meet these goals. One of the most challenging pieces of the planning process is to develop evaluation questions that can measure the achievement of goals.

The word "measurement" implies the use of numbers or quantitative data, but qualitative data can be equally important in the summative evaluation process. Creating precise and measurable evaluation questions is one of the most critical activities you will undertake, because questions drive the data collection, analysis, and reporting processes.

The goals of the AMB project were stated in the grant proposal. Through the use of AMB equipment, training, and ongoing support, school teachers/ staff will improve academic success for at-risk students with print disabilities by providing them access to grade level curriculum via audiobooks.

The project will also reduce antisocial behavior on the part of these students as a result of their greater engagement in classroom academic activities. The evaluation questions AMB derived from the goals were:

1. How are audiobooks used in schools served by the grant?
2. To what extent do teachers and administrators in these schools improve their awareness and knowledge of the potential contribution of audiobooks?
3. To what extent do teachers see academic and behavioral benefits from audiobook use among students with print disabilities, that is those with low vision and those with learning issues, such as dyslexia?
4. To what extent do students using audiobooks perceive academic and behavioral changes in themselves?

Step Two: Collecting Information. The second task in the evaluation process comprises collecting the information you need. For each evaluation question, you need to determine the best sources of information. Some data are readily available, but other information will need to be collected from primary sources through interviews and surveys.

Programs usually leave a trail of paper; the challenge lies in identifying which documents will yield useful information. A good first step is to make a list of all the documents available, unofficial as well as official, and note the general types of information that may be gleaned from each.

Document analysis can shed light on past and present program activities and processes. For example, you can categorize meeting topics and issues, such as planning training sessions, recruitment, and budget, to reveal how the program management and steering committee are likely to spend their time. What issues seem to recur; what questions seem to remain unresolved over a series of meetings?

The AMB program was unusual in that little documentation existed because it was a pilot program in an area where the agency had little direct prior experience. The only available program documentation at the beginning of the evaluation was the grant proposal, which was well written and detailed.

The participating schools' websites provided demographic data that confirmed that the program served students specifically targeted by the grant: minority, special education, and low income.

- School A was 54 percent minority, 22 percent special education, and 38 percent low income.
- School B was 84 percent minority, 23 percent special education, and 65 percent low income.
- School C was 92 percent minority, 18 percent special education students, and 76 percent low income.

To collect quantitative data about key issues, surveys are an optimal choice. Online survey tools have made this activity much easier than the traditional pencil-and-paper questionnaire. Nevertheless, they are not foolproof; in survey design, the devil is absolutely in the details. To assure you obtain usable and complete responses:

- Make sure the instructions for completing the survey are clear and succinct.
- Set a firm date for completing the survey.
- Don't ask leading questions; that is, questions that imply what the response should be.
- Don't assume too much about what respondents know. (For example, don't use acronyms; spell out the name of any organization to which you refer.)

Take the time to format the questionnaire for readability and ease of response. Group questions into categories. Then, pilot test the survey questions by asking several individuals to complete the survey and give you feedback on what worked and what didn't.

The most common source of qualitative data is interviews, whether in person or on the telephone. The responses from the interviews allow you to view a program or an activity in depth from another person's viewpoint. By asking open-ended questions, listening attentively, taking notes, and asking follow-up questions, you can get a rich, detailed picture of the program.

Identify a list of questions or issues to be explored during each interview. It is important that these questions be open-ended, so that interviewees have the opportunity to speak freely and openly. Don't ask questions that can be answered "yes" or "no." If the respondent simply answers "no," you are at a dead end. "To what extent" is a good way to start a question to avoid this trap.

Interviews can produce anecdotes or vignettes that will enliven your report and bring out the effects of the program on individuals. People like to read stories and tend to remember them.

A particularly useful type of personal interview is called the "Key Informant Interview." To use this technique, identify experts on the program, such as people who manage similar programs and people who are knowledgeable about the community context. If the program designers are available, they can provide valuable history and context.

Occasionally, it may be useful to interview a "Hostile Informant," someone who is opposed to the program. This perspective may actually help to identify program issues or to understand the barriers preventing successful implementation. It may also serve to defuse the hostility. Once informants discuss their grievances, they feel they have not been heard nor addressed.

Focus-group interviews are organized group discussions that focus on particular issues or themes, such as recruiting participants, or how well the program is meeting the needs of a particular constituency. The benefit of having a group discussion is that participants can build upon one another's ideas.

The goal of the focus group interview is not to reach consensus, but rather to explore the range of viewpoints. Focus groups typically consist of between six and eight participants, a moderator, and a recorder. The interview usually lasts one to two hours. Due to the number of people involved and the limited amount of time, the moderator must have a list of questions prepared in advance.

As a general rule of thumb, a moderator can hope to cover four to six questions in a session lasting an hour and a half. To conduct successful focus-group interviews:

- At the beginning of the session, create a neutral, nonintimidating environment that helps participants to express their ideas freely.
- Ensure that all individuals have the opportunity to participate and that no one dominates the discussion.
- At the beginning of the session, state the purpose of the questions, the length of the session, and a general time limit for responding to each question.
- Emphasize that there are no right or wrong answers.
- Record and transcribe the focus-group interview whenever possible.

If it is not possible to record or no permission is given to record, then take the best notes you can and jot down the responses that come to mind right after the event. Better yet, have a second person take notes.

Observations of an activity, class, or event can provide rich, descriptive information about the program context and individual characteristics and activities. For example, nonverbal communications, patterns of interaction, and participant behaviors reveal important insights as to the inner workings of a program.

If your observation focuses on a specific issue, create a checklist of the behaviors that are relevant to the topic. For example, these topics were part of a checklist for quality of teacher instruction in a high-school classroom. The teacher:

• Responds directly to questions and comments;
• Gives overview when opening a new topic, subject, or activity;
• Gives clear instructions/procedures for doing activities; and
• Gives summaries at the end of a discussion, presentation, or activity.

If the purpose of your observation is not a specific issue, keep running notes but do not attempt to interpret the information. Keep in mind that written descriptions should be detailed enough so another reader can get an accurate picture of what has occurred.

AMB's program involved twenty-two teachers and their students in three schools. Although ideally the data collection would entail two sources of evidence for each evaluation question, AMB did not have the resources to conduct observations or focus groups. However, they selected the data sources that were tied closely to specific evaluation issues.

Step Three: Analyzing and Reporting. Analysis of the information does not need to be a highly technical task. Use data from several sources or data that has been collected in a variety of ways;—for example, surveys, focus groups, observations—to address each evaluation question.

If you organize the findings by research question it will be easier for your audience to review, analyze, and synthesize the information. Also, if the program is being implemented in more than one location, present data by site in order to see variations in the degree of implementation or extent of successful outcomes.

The AMB materials were used in different settings across the schools that participated in the program. The evaluation report provided a summary of the users in each school. For example, audiobooks were used:

• By mainstream classroom and special education teachers in class or for homework;

- In the resource room;
- In the library;
- In afterschool tutorials; and
- In required independent reading.

Change in teacher knowledge was documented by a survey of the teachers who attended training provided by a member of the program staff. Twenty-two teachers (100 percent) of the respondents somewhat agreed or strongly agreed that "The training increased my understanding of audiobook utilization." Asked if they were more likely to use audiobooks because of the training, 95 percent of teachers agreed that they would.

Questions concerning the academic and social benefits to their students were addressed by a second teacher survey and thirteen interviews. The survey was administered before classroom implementation took place, which was not ideal but was the only time possible.

The first item on the AMB teacher survey asked if there were students in their schools who are at risk partly due to their inability to access the curriculum. Ninety-five percent of teachers agreed or strongly agreed with this statement. There was unanimous agreement among teachers that audio textbooks "may benefit some" of these students.

Interviews with thirteen teachers and administrators at the conclusion of the program, which spanned one academic year, focused on the benefits of audiobooks in terms of academic and social change in students. The academic benefits cited were access to the curriculum, reading comprehension, and an increased willingness and ability of students with special needs to participate in class.

The educators who were interviewed spoke of behavioral benefits for students as well. In general, students using audiobooks were less likely to be distracted, more able to focus, and thus more likely to behave appropriately in the classroom. Quotations from these interviews enriched understanding of the social benefits to students.

"Students using the audiobooks are more likely to participate in class and they show improved ability to finish their work. Overall, students have an increased investment in the work and more confidence." In another interview, a faculty member said his own son with learning disabilities was " 'a changed child.' He is reading and listening along. He is doing much better in his homework."

A survey administered near the end of the school year tapped into students' feelings about using audiobooks. Of the sixteen students who responded, 94 percent said that using the audiobooks helped them "learn a lot" or were "sometimes helpful." A full 100 percent reported that using audiobooks helped them understand their schoolwork all or most of the time. There was no funding for standardized testing to confirm reading gains.

Step Four: Reflecting on the Meaning of Information. The final phase of the evaluation is the most important and the most frequently overlooked. All the work that has gone into planning and conducting the evaluation is useless if the report just ends up sitting on a shelf.

Some suggestions for activities that generate reflection and might be used by any relevant group such as managers, staff, teachers, advisors, and participants include text rendering and reflective conversation. Each activity provides time for individual reflection, sharing, and group discussion.

Text Rendering is a technique in which each person selects and underlines one sentence from the evaluation report that stands out as particularly important. Each then reads the selected sentence aloud to the group.

This reading is uninterrupted; the person reading does not explain or comment on the sentence. No one else in the group asks a question or comments until after everyone has read a sentence. When the rendering is complete, the discussion begins with such questions as: What were patterns or themes in the sentences selected? Why do these seem to be important?

Another technique is called Reflective Conversation. The group agrees on a phrase or finding that seems important to understanding the implications of the evaluation results. Each member of the group writes notes reflecting on the meaning, associations, and importance of the phrase and then reads the notes to the group.

The group then engages in reflective discussion of what people learned. After these activities, the group turns its attention to the question: What are the implications of the evaluation and our discussions?

PITFALLS IN THE EVALUATION PROCESS

Under the pressure of getting the program up and running and facing daily challenges, the program manager may fall into unproductive evaluation habits or pitfalls. To avoid pitfalls, be attentive to the following:

Collect Baseline Data. Any program needs to know the characteristics of its participants and what they are doing. That sounds very basic, but it often proves to be a stumbling block, especially when multiple organizations are implementing a program or when a program operates in several locations.

Obtain Timely Data. Organizations that provide services to your program need to be encouraged to provide data to the evaluation in a timely manner. They already have their own paperwork to deal with and records to keep so it helps to provide a template or outline that makes reporting easier and assures that the information is consistent.

Counting Things. A great temptation in undertaking self-evaluation is to count things; for example, how many workshops were given, how many people attended, how many copies of the materials were circulated. There is nothing wrong with counting things, but it has limited usefulness to an evaluation.

The easiest things to tally are accomplishments, rather than outcomes. Accomplishments may be defined as things totally under your control, and outcomes as things that go beyond your control. For example, if you say, "I want to give six workshops" and then you give six workshops, that is an accomplishment. If, on the other hand, you say, "I want to give six workshops that will assist the participants to become more effective leaders," then you have introduced an outcome element.

Another reason that people count things is that they believe that the most important aspects of what they are doing cannot be measured. How do you measure an "effective leader?" Stymied, program managers may give up on evaluating the important things and end up reporting what is easily measurable, whether it is important or not.

Actually, although you can't measure leadership directly; you can measure characteristics and demonstrations of effective leadership. These include such things as initiating actions, attention to detail, and understanding the big picture of the program. You may also elicit the opinions of those who work with and for the leader of the program.

Nonnegotiables. Every program represents the ideal of the people who designed it. However, the implementation of a program, that is the point where ideals meet realities, seldom matches the design exactly. If you don't define your nonnegotiables at the beginning, you may negotiate away key premises of the program design.

For example, if the program design includes three connected components and the designers believe it is crucial for participants to take part in all three, then that becomes a nonnegotiable feature of the program. If you then allow some participants to enroll in only one or two components, you no longer have the same program; its integrity is compromised and any evidence of success is conflated.

Learning from the Information. Research has repeatedly demonstrated that a program's success is closely linked to its ability to look systematically at information about itself, to reflect about what that information means, and to build future program efforts around what it has learned from experience. Yet there is also research that suggests that few people in an organization learn anything from an evaluation and those who do, learn very little.

Perhaps the reason for disinterest in the results is that evaluation is seen by many practitioners as an alien activity. At an evaluation workshop, the program directors of multiple sites of a federally funded initiative were asked to do a word-association exercise, using the word "evaluation." The most common responses were "intrusive," "time-consuming," "frightening," and "not useful."

To overcome that kind of fear and anxiety, building in some components of evaluation from the beginning of the program may open the eyes of the staff to the usefulness of collecting information. The program director might ask the staff members: What do you want to know about the participants? How will you judge if an activity is working? What do you think might hamper the success of our program?

Once the staff connects the idea of what they want to know with the concept of evaluation, you are halfway there. The rest consists of designing the tools such as surveys and interview protocols to collect the information that they themselves have decided is important. You will have also realized the basic premise of evaluation, which is that knowledge convincingly proves the success of programs or, if the program is not very successful, the evidence helps you understand where it fell short and why.

CONCLUSIONS

Vision as Catalyst

Chapter 14

Conclusion

Henry Wadsworth Longfellow[1] said, "I shot an arrow into the air. It fell to earth I know not where." And so, the education establishment continues to drop program interventions onto schools, and schools continue to drop education on students. And that's not okay. The students and their families deserve better and the leaders of the education establishment at all levels must take responsibility for the way things are and the changes they can make if they have the will to do so.

Educators need to realize that today's students are different. The culture they grow up in is different. Their families are different. Dick and Jane, Spot and Puff are gone and won't be back. It still takes a village to raise a child, but in the culture of modern poverty, intact families are rare and isolation is the norm, the schools must become the village. It is up to the schools to provide a sense of belonging and connections that children desperately need to thrive and succeed.

We not only fail to educate children in poverty, but in many cases we stifle their desire to learn. They begin school hopeful and leave school cynical. We punish poverty with dirty schools, inadequate resources, incompetent teachers, and complacent principals whose dearest wish is to maintain the status quo, hoping their test scores will, like Lazarus from the dead, rise without any effort on their part.

The national narrative of public education increasingly becomes a story of power and the lack of it. Sadly, those in the establishment who have power may yield to the temptation to misuse it, while the students and their families, who have the largest stake in the system, remain powerless. Yet every student who comes to school wants to learn and every parent, no matter how broken their own lives have become, wants their child to succeed.

The problems in education are complex, pervasive, and challenging and the solutions of the past have seldom been very effective, but what if the approach was turned inside out and upside down? What about creating a school that is worthy of the students and the families who become part of it?

When a child comes to public school at the age of four or five, it is not just his or her little academic self who arrives; it is a whole package of personality, potential, and early experiences. Some children already bear a heavy burden of experiences that they should never have had. Some have been nurtured and sheltered.

Some have already had to fend for themselves. Some have library cards; others have never owned a book nor seen an adult read one. If they are poor or have disabilities, or their parents don't speak English, they are likely to become second-rate citizens in a third-rate system.

Although some are bruised and some do not shine, nature does not produce bad apples nor bad children. From that first day at school, the education system has twelve years to help students to realize their potential and to produce informed citizens who understand their responsibilities in a democracy. It is the task, the challenge, and the privilege, of public schools to fulfill their responsibilities in the process.

The American public education enterprise resembles a giant galley ship. On the top deck are the affluent children of the suburban schools with their parents arrayed around them, protecting and advocating for them. The teachers on this deck are generally effective and they have the needed physical and technical resources. Below decks, chained to the oars of the galley, are the children whose parents are too poor, too ill educated, or too powerless to take on the system and free their children.

CREATING SCHOOLS ON A FRAMEWORK OF VISIONS

Schoolwide visions are shared beliefs in the perfectibility of the system. You may not realize all the visions, but making progress toward them makes the school better for the students, their families, and the teachers. If you are the principal, you inculcate the visions into all the teachers, including the new ones. If they don't understand the language of visions, they probably shouldn't teach in your school.

You talk about the visions in faculty meetings, with families at Back to School Night, or at the PTO. You discuss the visions with students as soon as they are old enough to understand the concept, which is probably younger than you first believe. When visitors ask what is unique about this school, everyone responds "We live by our visions."

Establish Connectedness. The foundation of the framework of visions is that every student in the school belongs to the school community. That means the special education students, the quiet students, the students with anger issues, and the students who seem to be loners or are difficult to reach. Connectedness, community, and a sense of belonging are critically important to helping students to succeed socially and academically.

Beyond that, a sense of belonging to a caring school community may be the best prevention of the kind of violence that has lately beset American schools. Becoming an inclusive, caring community is the single most important change any school can make.

Example from Practice. It sometimes takes so little to make a difference. In one middle school, the principal had decreed that all teachers greet their students individually as they filed into their homerooms. Every student got a handshake, a smile, and a few encouraging words. Sam, glowering, tried to get past the teacher, but he could not ignore her outstretched hand. "Wow," she said, "It's only eight o'clock and you already look like you are having a very bad day." Sam mumbled his reply, but the teacher kept hold of his hand while she said, "Let's turn it around right here. Let's make it a very good day, OK?" His face cleared and he smiled reluctantly as he ambled into the classroom.

Develop a Consensus of Visions. A convergence of visions is the foundation of education. Schools grant the right of differing dreams of what is best for the student and give students and their families opportunities to express them. The school holds everyone's vision to be valid and works to establish a consensus.

Honor Aspirations. In a school based on visions, families and students are encouraged to work toward their highest dreams of the future, not with a guarantee that they will achieve all their ideals, but with the assurance that they have the right to aspire. The school's task is to help students to achieve their aspirations by holding them to challenging academic standards and offering appropriate academic supports.

Make Families Welcome. Many of the families of today's students look and experience life differently than a generation ago, but they care about their children just as much. The schoolwide vision must include every family as part of the school community. Families are not part of the problem; families are a critical part of the solution.

Establish a climate in which families can have lunch with their children and visit classes. Give students and families opportunities to provide honest feedback on every aspect of the educational process.

TREAT EVERY STUDENT AS AN INDIVIDUAL

Every child has special gifts and every child has some special needs. The corollary of course is that every child needs an individualized education plan or IEP. The student who squints at the board or the book will probably be referred for a vision test. The student who can't stay still and focus will probably be referred for testing for an attention deficit disorder. But what about all the others? The quiet ones, the obedient ones who don't make any trouble? How do we know as soon as possible what they can do and what challenges them?'

Many schools, especially those serving the poorest students, are deficit-driven, focusing on what students don't know and can't do. Every school has a special education program, but few have programs of enrichment for gifted students. Research tells us that intellectually gifted students exist in impoverished schools in about the same proportion as in more affluent schools. Gifted students also need IEPs.

Example from Practice. A student in a focus group of eighth graders said that he never told his teacher that he had finished his work. "If I do, she'll give me another worksheet or ask me to help another kid with his work. I'm not the teacher, she is." Another student volunteered, "I read fast and as soon as I look up from the book, the teacher points at me and says, 'Read it again!'"[2]

Another Example from Practice. A school board member in a rural district admitted that it was expensive to maintain a program for gifted students, but it was worth it. "When I'm old and sitting in a rocking chair, it will be a better rocking chair because one of these students will invent it."

A plan developed at the end of kindergarten and revisited at the end of the first grade and again at the end of third grade will determine if the students need to be part of a gifted program, if they need additional help, or if they display troubling problems. The end of third grade is a watershed for students. If their academic and emotional problems are not discovered by that time, it will become more and more difficult to do so.

The only true nonnegotiable in the early primary grades is that every student who is capable of doing so must learn to read. If they can't learn to read, these young students need help immediately because they have no chance of success in the upper grades without reading skills.

SUMMING IT UP

The reason to begin the change process by focusing on visions is that people can embrace a new perspective from visions. They can see themselves inside a vision much more than they can envision themselves as a part of a system. Although the phrase commonly used is "systemic change," the reality is that it is human change. That change begins with you and me and all the rest of us who understand the urgency of making school the place where students learn academic skills, life skills, and the joy of a productive life.

NOTES

1. Henry W. Longfellow, "The Arrow and the Song," www.hwlongfellow.org/poems_front.php. (Accessed November 19, 2018.)

2. P. Olszewski-Kubilius, et al., "Where Are the Gifted Minorities?" http://www.davidsongifted.org/Search-database/A10759.

Appendix

Your Toolbox

The survey forms and interview protocols included in this section are intended to help administrators and teachers discover information vital to decision making. Two types of tools comprise the toolbox. The first set is focused on seeing the school through the eyes of students. The Shadowing Protocol and the Kids with Cameras activity provide a way to explore this overlooked dimension of schools, and the student experience.

The other set of tools taps into feelings and attitudes that are often left unsaid but are nonetheless powerful influences on teachers' and families' action and behavior. Learning about the teachers' view of professional development will assist in closing the gap between what teachers want from professional development and what they may need but find difficult to accept.

Special education is a large component of education and is one where people's feelings and attitudes may be suppressed. Family members who find the IEP meeting intimidating and teachers who are dubious about the inclusion of students with disabilities in their classroom both hinder the development of a partnership between schools and families.

All the tools are also available per request to nbrighamassoc@yahoo.com.

STUDENT SHADOWING PROTOCOL FOR USE IN MIDDLE AND HIGH SCHOOLS

Purposes of Shadowing Students

Shadowing is a methodology that consists of following a single student through one or more school day(s) and documenting the student's experiences and interactions. Shadowing is intended to: (1) describe aspects of the school experience that affect individual children needs, including patterns of instruction, access to academics, and instructional quality; and (2) examine instruction as received, that is, from the students' perspective.

Benefits of Shadowing Students

School board members will learn about important issues of curriculum, school climate, and quality of instruction. District administrators will see the context of an intervention before deciding to implement any new program. Members of advocacy groups, for example, special education, will acquire a deeper understanding of issues affecting students with disabilities.

Selection of Students to Shadow

Choosing students to Shadow is a critical part of the process. As a general rule, select students that represent your area of interest, special education students, students in gifted or accelerated programs, or students identified as being at risk. You can also select students at random if your interest is in broader areas such as school climate or patterns of instruction.

An Essential Question as the Basis for Shadowing

Shadowing is most effective when you start with an essential question, the most important thing you want to know. It might be "How is a student engaged with learning in this school?" or "What are the patterns of instruction in this school?" For example, how much time is spent in rote learning or individual seatwork? How do teachers respond to students' questions? How do teachers present instructions, for example, do they share the purpose of the lesson or offer opportunities for students to work together?

Prerequisites for Shadowing

In order to undertake a Shadowing experience, you need permission from the school principal and the teachers being observed. Depending on district policy, you may also need permission from the parent or guardian of the Shadowed student. You don't need formal permission from the student, but an introductory conversation about who you are and why you are Shadowing him or her is a courtesy. Most students will be excited about the special attention. Make sure to answer the student's questions before you start.

The Process and the Protocol

Complete a separate protocol for each academic class/lesson that the student attends during the day. On entering the class, introduce yourself to the teacher, thank him or her for agreeing to have you observe the student in the class, and explain that the focus is on the student and is not an evaluation of the teacher. Note the following general information at the beginning of each observation. Take detailed notes to address the subsequent questions.

General Information:
Student Name
Teacher Name
Subject
Grade Level
Beginning Time
End Time

For each lesson:

What is the objective of the lesson?

• Is an objective for the lesson written on the board?
• Does the teacher state the objective of the lesson at the beginning of class?
• Is the lesson continued from the previous day? If so, does the teacher remind students of the important ideas from the earlier lesson?

What is the flow of the lesson?

• Does the teacher vary the activities during the class or do students do the same thing throughout the class period?
• In what ways and how often does the Shadowed student interact with the teacher(s)?
• Does the Shadowed student have an opportunity to work with peers, such as participating in a group activity?
• If there is seatwork, does the student seem to understand and complete it in a timely manner?

To what extent is the Shadowed student engaged in the lesson?

• Does the student participate in class discussion?
• Does the student ask or respond to questions?
• Does the student ask for help and, if so, receive it from the teacher?

- Is the student involved in behavioral issues?
- Are there any interruptions during class that affect learning time, either from the outside or caused by student disruption?

Optional Interview Questions for Students (before class):

- What would you like to tell me about this class?
- What would you like to tell me about this teacher?
- What is easy/hard/interesting about this class?
- What's easy/hard about doing your homework for this class?
- Does the teacher help you with homework if you ask?

KIDS WITH CAMERAS

Purpose of Kids with Cameras

The purpose of Kids with Cameras is to discover what connects students to their schools. The tool can be useful to school boards members, district administrators, and family advocacy groups. The first question is a basic one: "What do you want to know?" You might want to know why certain types of students, like English language learners or special education students, are dropping out of school or why tenth-graders in one school are staying in school while in other schools they are dropping out.

You might be interested in assessing the general climate in one or more of your middle or high schools. Kids with Cameras can provide the student perspective to address these and many other questions.

How to Use This Tool

Kids with Cameras is straightforward and cost effective to implement. All that is needed is one or two teachers who are willing to take on the assignment, some digital or disposable cameras, and a cadre of students. Student selection is determined by the topic. Even students with severe disabilities can participate if accompanied by an adult as they take pictures.

Students need clear instructions and a time frame. Keep the instructions to a minimum but made it clear that only one or two pictures can be of friends. Ask the students to think about questions such as these.

- What adults are important to me in the school?
- What things are important to me in the school?

- What places are important to me in the school?
- What activities are important to me in the school?

Kids with Cameras works best if the students have no more than three days to complete the assignment and if they are given some out-of-class time to take the pictures. Select no more than fifteen students at a time to keep the project manageable.

Administering Kids with Cameras includes getting the pictures taken, collecting the cameras, having the pictures developed or put on a disc, and then scheduling an interview with each student. Alternatively, smartphone technology may be used, as long as all the students have smartphones.

The discussion with students is key to understanding why they took each picture and what it means for them. Do not attach the students' names to the pictures, but label them so that pictures from a single student can be identified. Be sure to get two sets of pictures from each camera so the students will have one to take home.

Reflecting on the meaning of information is the most important part of the process, but it is often rushed or overlooked. Encourage the group that sponsors the Kids with Cameras activity to devote at least one hour to review the students' pictures and interviews.

A culminating question could be, "What are the implications for action?" You don't have to consider every picture. Some will be blurred or out of focus and some will be clearly irrelevant. Once the pictures have been gathered and a narrative is attached to them, consider these questions:

- What themes or patterns emerge from the pictures selected?
- What do these patterns tell us about student connections to school?
- What are the implications of our discussion for further action?

The results of Kids with Cameras provide a new appreciation of the idea that knowledge is power. Knowing what connects students to school can generate ideas for building broader and stronger student connections.

SURVEY OF FAMILY MEMBERS' ATTITUDES TOWARD SCHOOL

Purpose

This survey taps into the feelings of family members about the extent to which they feel welcome in their child's school, and the extent to which teachers and school staff see them as partners in the education process. The survey is useful to school administrators and parent advocacy groups looking to increase meaningful family involvement.

Please Tell Us about Yourself.

A1. Your Gender   MALE ☐   FEMALE ☐

A2. Your Child's Gender   MALE ☐   FEMALE ☐

A3. Your Race

    AFRICAN AMERICAN _____

    CAUCASIAN _____

    LATINO/LATINA _____

    ASIAN _____

    NATIVE AMERICAN _____

A4. I am this child's

    MOTHER   ☐

    FATHER   ☐

    OTHER RELATIVE   ☐

    LEGAL GUARDIAN   ☐

Care and Respect at This School

B1. Please tell us how these statements describe your experience with this school.

	Yes	No	Not Sure
a. I feel welcome when I go to the school.			
b. I am respected by the teachers and others at the school.			
c. My child is respected by teachers and others at the school.			
d. The teachers and other people at the school care about my child's future.			
e. My child feels like he/she belongs in this school.			

SURVEY OF TEACHER ATTITUDES TOWARD THE INCLUSION OF STUDENTS WITH DISABILITIES

Purpose

The purpose of this survey is to determine the attitudes of teachers toward including inclusion of students with disabilities in their classrooms. It is valuable for setting school policy and planning professional development. The survey is set up as a computer-based instrument but may be used on paper.

The Survey Instrument

Thank you for taking the time to answer these survey questions. Your responses will provide valuable information to help understand your current teaching practices and your perceptions of how your school addresses students with disabilities. The survey is also intended to find out how supported you feel in addressing the learning needs of these students. All your responses will be kept confidential.

Your candid opinions and responses are valued and appreciated. For the purposes of this survey, students with disabilities are defined as students with mild to moderate learning needs requiring some additional support and curriculum modification.

Which of the following best describes your position in your school?
- ☐ General education teacher
- ☐ Special education teacher
- ☐ Teaching assistant
- ☐ Paraprofessional
- ☐ Tutor
- ☐ Counselor
- ☐ Therapist
- ☐ Other (Specify): _____

What grade(s) do you teach? (Check all that apply.)
- ☐ Kindergarten
- ☐ 1st grade
- ☐ 2nd grade
- ☐ 3rd grade
- ☐ 4th grade
- ☐ 5th grade
- ☐ 6th grade
- ☐ 7th grade

☐ 8th grade
☐ 9th grade
☐ 10th grade
☐ 11th grade
☐ 12th grade
☐ Other (Specify): _____

What subject(s) do you teach? (Check all that apply.)
☐ Language Arts
☐ Mathematics
☐ Science
☐ Social Studies
☐ Technology/Computer Science
☐ Visual Arts
☐ Music
☐ Other (Specify): _____

How long have you been teaching?
☐ Less than 3 years
☐ 3–9 years
☐ 10–20 years
☐ 21 years or more

How long have you been teaching at your current school?
☐ Less than 3 years
☐ 3–9 years
☐ 10–20 years
☐ 21 years or more

What is your highest degree earned?
☐ BA/BS
☐ MA or MEd
☐ EdD or PhD
☐ Other (specify): _____

What is your gender?
☐ Female
☐ Male

Please provide some information about your experience teaching students with disabilities.

To what extent do you encounter students with disabilities (SWD) in the classes you teach? (Check one.)

☐ Never or I'm not aware of any SWD in my classes. (If checked, go to the last question.)

☐ One or two SWD on average per class.

☐ Three to six SWD on average per class.

☐ More than six SWD on average per class.

Do you currently use any of the following strategies to accommodate SWD learning? (Check all that apply.)

☐ I don't use any special strategies to accommodate their learning.

☐ Differentiated instruction.

☐ Small-group instruction (homogeneous).

☐ Small-group instruction (heterogeneous).

☐ Assistive technologies (e.g., computer-based instruction, books on tape, etc.).

☐ Assistive devices (e.g., keyboards, large-print texts).

☐ One-on-one instruction (e.g., by teacher, an instructional aide, or tutor).

☐ Modified assignments.

☐ Extra time for assessments.

☐ Other (specify):

On average, how often do you design lessons and use strategies that specifically accommodate students with special learning needs in your classes? (Check one.)

☐ Once a month

☐ Once a week

☐ Several times a week

☐ Daily

☐ Other (Specify): _____

To date, have you been provided with any resources or support from your school administrators or outside agencies to assist you in teaching SWD? (Check all that apply.)

☐ No resources have been provided

☐ Speech and language therapists

☐ Occupational therapists

☐ Learning specialists

☐ Instructional assistants

☐ Paraprofessionals

☐ Tutors

☐ Other (Specify): _____

In the past year, have you participated in any professional development specifically addressing instructional strategies for students with disabilities? (Check all that apply.)

☐ I did not participate in any professional development activities addressing SWD.

☐ National or statewide conferences

☐ Regional workshops or conferences

☐ Online webinars

☐ Courses specifically addressing SWD at universities or colleges

☐ In-school retreats or workshops

☐ Job-embedded and individual coaching or mentoring

☐ Teacher-led collaborative learning teams (e.g., study groups, learning communities, or professional communities of practice).

☐ Other (specify): _____

Do you agree or disagree with the following statements regarding the learning of students with disabilities?

	Agree	Disagree	No Opinion
All students prefer to be in classes where students with diverse learning needs are served.	1	2	3
Teaching all students regardless of learning needs in one classroom increases enthusiasm and motivation for learning among all students.	1	2	3
Teaching students regardless of learning needs in one classroom increases socialization and a sense of school cohesion among all students.	1	2	3
Teaching all students regardless of learning needs in the same classroom encourages all students to engage in higher-level thinking skills.	1	2	3

Thank you for your time and thoughtful responses to this survey.

TEACHERS' RETROSPECTIVE JUDGMENT OF THE USEFULNESS OF PROFESSIONAL DEVELOPMENT

Purpose

Likert Scale surveys are traditional evaluation tools administered at the end of workshops and other professional development activities. A standard question on these surveys is, "Do you think you will use the information and materials in your work?" A positive response on this question indicates in part the enthusiasm of the moment. It may not be a true appraisal of the likelihood of actual implementation.

By contrast, the use of the Retrospective Judgment interview protocol allows a deeper probing at a subsequent time when respondents have had the opportunity to reflect on the extent to which the event has changed their thinking or influenced their work.

How to Use

Immediately following the professional-development event, participants are asked if they would be willing to talk in greater depth about their experience at a later time and, if so, to provide their names and phone/email addresses. The calls will take place at least thirty days after the event and are of twenty- to thirty-minutes duration.

The Telephone Interview Protocol

After introducing yourself and explaining the purpose of the interview, say:
"I understand that you attended the (name of event) on (date of event)."
If the respondent does not remember at first, add other information, such as the name of the presenter or the theme of the event.
- What was the key message of the event that you remember now?
- To what extent did the event change your perspective on instruction or add to your personal knowledge on the topic?
- What new skills or strategies did you acquire? (If appropriate.)
- To what extent have you used what you learned from the event in your classroom instruction?
- Are these new skills, strategies, or materials something that you intend to use in your classroom on a regular basis?
- If not used: why did you decide not to use the skills/strategies/materials? (Probe for not appropriate, not high quality, too much preparation required, not enough support from trainers.)

Final question regardless of use or nonuse:

• What are your suggestions for improving future, similar professional events?

TEACHER ASSESSMENT OF THE QUALITY OF PROFESSIONAL DEVELOPMENT ACTIVITY

Purpose

Professional development is expensive in both financial cost and the time teachers are out of the classroom to participate. This survey may be used by administrators at the school or district level to assess the extent to which teachers found that a recent professional-development experience engaged them and met their needs.

Quality Factors	True for None of the Activities	True for Some of the Activities	True for All of the Activities	Unable to Determine Or Not Applicable
	(Check one option for each quality factor)			
a. The trainer was knowledgeable and experienced in the topic presented.				
b. The trainer referenced current research and best practice in the field of the topic presented.				
c. Training directly addressed the needs of my classroom.				

d. The content of the training was concrete enough to apply directly to my classroom practice.				
e. Materials necessary to implement the new skill or strategy (e.g., books, articles, handouts, technologies) were readily available.				
f. The trainer used experiential or active learning techniques that engaged my interest.				
g. Technology was utilized that was appropriate to the topic (e.g., video, PowerPoint, Internet).				
h. Opportunities to practice new skills were part of the training.				
i. Participants had opportunities to network with colleagues.				
j. Opportunities for team-based learning were provided.				

k. Information and materials (e.g., website links) were provided to enable me to pursue topics further.				
l. All participants had an opportunity to ask questions and provide feedback on the training.				

MAKE YOUR SCHOOL A WELCOMING PLACE

Purpose

The purpose of this assessment is to determine the extent to which a school presents a welcoming environment for visitors. The first impression made by a school will influence visitors' attitudes toward all aspects of the school climate. A welcoming school particularly benefits visitors whose first language is not English and those adults who have unpleasant memories of their own school years.

Filling Out the Assessment

Anyone can complete this assessment, but the most unbiased observers are insiders/outsiders, such as school board members, members of the PTO, or a student advocacy group.

The Assessment Questions

- Is the entrance accessible for persons with physical handicaps or is an alternative physically accessible entrance clearly indicated?
  Yes ☐   No ☐
- Does signage clearly indicate which is the correct door for visitors to use?
  Yes ☐   No ☐
- If the main door is locked, does someone answer the intercom in a timely manner?
  Yes ☐   No ☐

- Is the lobby or area directly inside the school neat and welcoming?
  Yes ☐   No ☐
- Does the lobby display student work, trophies, or other indications that this is a community of learners?
  Yes ☐   No ☐
- Are hallways free of debris, such as broken chairs or discarded paper?
  Yes ☐   No ☐
- Do signs clearly indicate directions to the main office?
  Yes ☐   No ☐
- If signage is available, are signs in the major languages of the student population?
  Yes ☐   No ☐
- Is there a comfortable space for visitors to sit in another room or in the main office while waiting to meet with an administrator?
  Yes ☐   No ☐
- If the waiting area is in the main office, is it separate from students who are sick or who are being disciplined?
  Yes ☐   No ☐
- Does the visible front-office staff represent the diversity of students?
  Yes ☐   No ☐
- Is there someone in the office or someone readily available who can translate for parents and family members?
  Yes ☐   No ☐
- Is the front-office staff friendly, welcoming, and helpful to visitors?
  Yes ☐   No ☐
- Is there a policy for meeting hours, so that families know when and how to arrange meetings with teachers and administrators?
  Yes ☐   No ☐

About the Author

Nancy Brigham has worked in the field of education research for thirty-five years, primarily on issues of national significance. She has participated in congressionally mandated evaluations of programs such as Title 1 and Vocational Education and national studies commissioned by the National Science Foundation. She has also conducted evaluations for the Kellogg Foundation and the Lilly Endowment, as well as university-sponsored evaluations for Harvard University, MIT, and the Yale Child Development Center.

She owns and manages Nancy Brigham Associates (NBA), an education research and evaluation consulting firm founded in 1978 as Rosenblum Brigham Associates. The mission of NBA is to involve clients as partners in the evaluation process and to make concrete contributions to program improvement and student success.

A Fragile Enterprise is the culmination of thousands of hours Ms. Brigham has spent interviewing administrators, teachers, and families, as well as observing students through their whole school days. This book looks at education from the bottom up and documents a system that marginalizes failing schools and disenfranchises the students in greatest need.

Ms. Brigham attended Wheaton College, Norton, Massachusetts, and the Boston University Graduate School of Education. She resides in Lexington, Massachusetts.